BABUR

BABUR:

Diarist and Despot

S. M. EDWARDES, C.S.I., C.V.O.

GYAN

Published by

GYAN

Gyan Publishing House
5, Ansari Road
Daryaganj, New Delhi-110002
Phone: 011-47034999, 9811692060
E-mail: books@gyanbooks.com

Distribution Network
gyanbooks.com
India, USA, Canada, UK, Australia, France

ISBN : 978-81-212-9548-2 (PB)
First Published, 1926

2nd Impression 2023

Printed at: Gyan Press, Delhi.

BABUR
Author: S. M. EDWARDES

BABUR: DIARIST AND DESPOT

BABUR

Reproduced, with permission, from the original in the British Museum

BABUR: Diarist and Despot

By S. M. EDWARDES, C.S.I., C.V.O.

PREFACE

THIS sketch of the character of Zahir-ud-din Muhammad Babur Padshah is based almost entirely upon the most recent English translation of the *Babur-nama* (Memoirs of Babur) by Mrs. A. S. Beveridge, which was published by the Royal Asiatic Society in four fasciculi beween 1912 and 1921. As Mrs. Beveridge translated the record direct from the original Turki, her rendering reflects the Emperor's style more faithfully than the earlier translation by Leyden and Erskine of a Persian copy of the *Memoirs*. I have also consulted S. Lane-Poole's excellent study, *Babar*, in the Rulers of India Series (Clarendon Press). The quotations, the main facts, and the various episodes illustrating Babur's character are taken direct from Mrs. Beveridge's work, including her illuminating notes and appendices.

My thanks are due to the authorities of the British Museum, to the Secretary and Director,

Victoria and Albert Museum, South Kensington, and to the Librarian, India Office, for permission to reproduce the portraits of Babur and the pictures of his grave and burial garden in Kabul.

S. M. E.

CONTENTS.

ILLUSTRATIONS

CHRONOLOGY OF BABUR'S LIFE.

1483.—February 14th—Birth of Babur.

1488.—Babur is taken on a visit to Samarkand and there betrothed to his cousin Ayesha, daughter of Sultan Ahmad (Alacha) Khan.

1494.—June—Succeeds his father, Umar Shaikh, as King of Farghana.

1495.—Recovers Asfara and Khujand from Ahmad Mirza.

1497.—May—Expedition against Samarkand.

1497.—November—Babur takes Samarkand. Spends a hundred days there and leaves it to recover Farghana, seized in his absence by Tambal. Is ousted from all his possessions except the town of Khujand. Wanderings among Ailak shepherds.

1498.—Ali Dost restores Marghinan to Babur.

1499.—June—Babur recovers Farghana. Marries Ayesha.

1500.—Babur forced to sign treaty whereby Farghana is divided between himself and his brother Jahangir.

1500.—June—The Tarkhan family invite Babur to recapture Samarkand, but Shaibani Uzbeg forestalls him.

1500.—November—Babur seizes Samarkand from the Uzbegs.

1501.—May—Babur defeated by Shaibani Uzbeg in battle of Sar-i-pul.

1501.—July—Babur's first child, a daughter, born in Samarkand and dies about a month after birth.

1501.—May to November—Babur besieged in Samarkand by Shaibani.

1501.—December—Babur capitulates.

1502.—January to May—Babur wanders homeless in the hills with a few followers.

1502.—June—Seeks the protection of his uncle, Mahmud Khan, at Tashkend. Trooping of the Colours at Tashkend.

1502.—July—Participates with the Khans in attacking Tambal at Andijan. Takes Ush, Uzkend, and Marghinan, which are then handed over by the elder Khan to his younger brother. Tambal's brother, Bayazid, invites Babur to Akhsi.

1503.—January, February—Babur deserted by the Khans and attacked by Tambal. He flees to the Khans at Andijan.

1503.—June—Shaibani defeats the Khans at Akhsi, and Babur goes into exile in the hills south of Farghana.

1504.—June—Babur, with his brothers Jahangir and Nasir, his mother and others, starts for Khorasan, but changes his route and seeks Kabul.

1504.—October—Babur takes possession of Kabul.

1505.—January to May—Babur makes an expedition down the Khyber to Kohat; reaches the Indus; takes Ghazni. Expedition against the wild tribes of Afghanistan.

1506.—June—Sets out from Kabul with his army to support Sultan Husain of Herat against Shaibani Uzbeg.

1506.—October—After a march of 800 miles Babur meets the sons of Sultan Husain and spends a few weeks at Herat, the capital of Khorasan.

1506.—December 24th—Babur leaves Herat on return journey to Kabul. Terrible march through the snows.

1507.—Babur reaches Kabul. Seizes Kandahar from Shah Beg and Mukim. Mongol rebellion in Kabul.

1507-10.—Babur stays in Kabul, busy with administration. Letter received from Khan Mirza. Babur decides to attempt once again the conquest of Samarkand with the help of the Safavid Ruler of Persia, who had defeated Shaibani.

1511.—Battle with Uzbegs.

1511.—October—Babur again mounts the throne of Samarkand.

1512.—May—Babur relinquishes Samarkand for the last time.

1512.—November—Battle with Uzbegs at Ghazdivan. Defeat of Babur, who flies to Hisar and takes refuge in Kunduz.

1513 or 1514 (early).—Babur returns to Kabul.

1519.—Babur's first invasion of India. Takes Bajaur fort.

[1519-1526.—Five invasions of India; organisation of Kabul kingdom; suppression of Mongol revolt at Ghazni; conquest of Swat and Bajaur.]

1519.—February 17th—Fords the Indus. Secures submission of Bhira and the country between the Jhelum and Chinab. Takes chief town of Gakkars on way back to Kabul.

1520.—Third invasion of Hindustan. Attacks Gakkar tribe, quashes rebellion at Bhira and reaches Sialkot. Humayun appointed governor of Badakshan *vice* Khan Mirza deceased.

1522.—Shah Beg surrenders Kandahar to Babur.

1524.—Fourth invasion of India. Secures Lahore and the Punjab.

1525.—Babur ill with fever and dysentery.

1525.—November—Fifth invasion of India. Restores order in Panjab. Marches towards Delhi.

1526.—April 21st—Battle of Panipat. Babur defeats Ibrahim Lodi and occupies Delhi and Agra.

1527.—March 16th—Battle of Kanwaha. Defeat of Rana Sanga. Babur assumes title of *Ghazi.*

1528.—January 20th—Chanderi fort stormed.

1528-1530.—Pacification of Hindustan: northern India reduced to submission.

1530.—December 26th—Death of Babur at Agra.

CHAPTER I

A GREAT TIMURID

> "*Credo equidem, nec vana fides, genus esse deorum.*
> *Degeneres animos timor arguit.*"

CARLYLE has remarked in his *Heroes* that "Great men, taken up in any way, are profitable company,"—a saying which can be amply justified by a study of the romantic career of Zahir-ud-din Muhammad, surnamed Babur, the founder of the Mughal dynasty of India. In the records bequeathed by a vanished age he appears before us in the diverse rôles of ruler, warrior, sportsman, craftsman, author, penman, and devoted student of Nature; and as we turn the pages of the priceless *Memoirs*, in which he frankly discloses his hopes and fears, his thoughts and deeds, we realise that we are in the presence of one of the most human and attractive personalities that ever graced an Asiatic throne. That Babur's character should compel our admiration and respect is somewhat remarkable, in view of his direct descent from those two ruthless scourges of Central Asia, Chenghiz Khan and Timur or Tamerlane. But while he inherited their restless energy, he was endowed with certain finer qualities, which tempered and purified the savage characteristics of his barbarian ancestry.

Babur was the eldest son of Umar Shaikh Mirza, king of Farghana or, as it was later styled, Khokand, a Barlas Turk, who together with his brothers Ahmed Mirza and Mahmud Mirza formed a group of so-called Miranshahi Timurids. They owed this appellation, as well as their position, to the fact that their father, Abu Said, was a great-grandson of Timur. The other principal Timurid of Babur's day was Mirza Husein Baiqara of Herat, a great-great-grandson of Timur, who ruled the remnant of the Timurid empire in Khurasan, from Balkh to the Caspian Sea. Umar Shaikh's first wife, the mother of Babur, was Qutlug-nigar Khanum, the second daughter of Yunas Khan, who was descended direct from Chaghatai Khan, second son of the Mongol conqueror Chenghiz Khan. Thus through his Timurid father, Umar Shaikh, and his Chaghatai Mughal mother, Babur

UMAR SHAIKH ON A HUNTING EXPEDITION

Reproduced, with permission, from the original in the British Museum

inherited both "the courage and capacity of the Turk" and "the restless energy of the Mongol." Through his mother he was also related to Sultan Mahmud Khan of Tashkend, head of the Chaghatai Mughal hordes, and his brother Sultan Ahmad, the younger Khan, who were both sons of Yunas Khan. Another outstanding figure of the world of Babur's youth was the fierce Uzbeg leader, Shaibani or Shaibaq Khan, also a descendant of Chenghiz Khan, who had inherited in full measure the tenacity and fighting qualities of his notorious ancestor.

Among the many excellent character-sketches with which Babur has enlivened his autobiography, is one of his father, which clearly shows whence Babur acquired one or two of the more notable traits of his own nature. Umar Shaikh was "a short, stout, round-bearded and fleshy person," who used to fasten the strings of his tunic so tightly that they frequently tore away, when he puffed himself out: he cared little what he wore or what he ate; he drank heavily, was excellent company, and could recite poetry very well, albeit unable to compose a verse. He was amorously inclined, fond of draughts and dice-playing, a stout fighter and tolerably good archer, and could punch so hard that he never failed to fell a man with his fist. Towards the close of his life he largely relinquished wine-drinking for other forms of intoxicants, under the influence of which he sometimes lost his head: but except on such occasions he remained, as he always had been, "generous, affable, eloquent, daring and bold." His contempt for money and wealth, which Babur inherited, is well illustrated by his action after a pitched battle with the Uzbegs in Turkistan. Having crossed the frozen Urus river, he administered a sound beating to the enemy, who were on their way home from a profitable raid near Samarkand; and after setting aside their booty and prisoners, he restored the whole collection to its various owners, without coveting or retaining any portion whatever for himself. The curious manner in which he met his death is thus tersely recorded by Babur:—

> "The fort of Akhsi is situated above a deep ravine. Along this ravine stand the palace-buildings, and from it on

> Monday, Ramzan 4, Umar Sheikh flew, with his pigeons and their house, and became a falcon (i.e. soared from earth, died)."

In plain phrase, the royal pigeon-house suddenly subsided by accident down the precipice, carrying with it the ruler of Farghana, who, like his famous descendant Akbar, kept a large flock of tumbler pigeons and spent much of his leisure in watching their antics on the wing.

It was perhaps from his mother that Babur inherited much of his intellectual and artistic faculty. Her father, Yunas Khan, whose fine temper, good manners and conversational powers were widely acknowledged, was an expert calligraphist and excelled in painting and music. In the atmosphere of his court, which offered a welcome to learning and scholarship, Qutlug-nigar must have had every chance of adding to the knowledge derived from her early education, and, like other ladies of high family, was almost certainly a scholar of Turki and Persian, besides being well-versed in domestic accomplishments. Babur's two grandmothers—Aisan-daulat Begam and Shah Sultan Begam, his father's mother—must also have contributed to the moulding of his character. The latter, a highly accomplished woman, nurtured in the luxury of a wealthy home in Samarkand, may have taught him the secrets of social etiquette and the significance of the phrase *noblesse oblige;* while the former, born in the desert and inured to the rigours of a wild country, probably inspired the tenacity, the courage to face hardship, and the resolute self-reliance, which formed an integral feature of her grandson's character. The Mongols or Mughals of the pastoral steppes, to whom Aisan-daulat belonged, were by no means in favour socially with the polished, town-dwelling Turks of Timur's line, who, as Lane-Poole remarks, occupied themselves with the pleasures and profits of a governing class and had a horror of the discomforts of the nomad life. Their view is crystallised in a Persian verse, suspected to be the composition of Babur's son Humayun, which appears in the margin of one of the original copies of Babur's works:—

BABUR LAYING OUT A GARDEN

Reproduced, by permission, from the original painting in the Victoria and Albert Museum, South Kensington

Were the Mughal race angels, they would
be bad;
Written in gold, the name Mughal would
be bad;
Pluck not an ear from the Mughal's cornland,
What is sown with Mughal seed will be bad.

Of his native country, Farghana, Babur gives a full and charming description. The capital, Andijan, was prodigal of grain and fruit, especially melons, which, fresh or preserved, were an important item of Turki diet; while the pheasants "grow so surprisingly fat that rumour has it four people could not finish one they were eating with its stew." Overlooking the Andijan torrent were the gardens of Ush—Babur's special delight—bright with violets, tulips and roses, and watered by perennial streams. One particular field of clover was a favourite halting-place of travellers, who, if they were wise, resisted the temptation to fall asleep there; for, according to Babur, "the ragamuffins of Ush" were addicted to practical joking and thought nothing of turning the waters of the canal on to the sleeper. Kasan, too, was bright with gardens; Marghinan provided good hunting and fowling; pheasant, hare, and the Asiatic wapiti *(Cervus maral)* fell to the sportsman in Khujand. In most districts grapes, apricots and pomegranates flourished in abundance, vying in popularity with the melons of Akhsi, which were finer than the famous melons of Bukhara. Babur never forgot the melons of Farghana, and tells us how once at Kabul, after long years, his eyes filled with tears at the scent of a melon, which reminded him of his old home. Besides a bountiful soil, the country possessed mines of iron and turquoise, and was blest with a temperate and invigorating climate, save only in Khujand, where, according to popular report, "even the sparrows got fever." Set like a jewel between the snow-capped mountains of Badakshan and the wild northern country, wasted by Mughal and Uzbeg raiders, Farghana was in truth a delectable land of bumper harvests and fair gardens, capable under prudent management of supporting three or four thousand fighting men.

Such were the influences, personal and climatic, that surrounded Babur's childhood. They confirmed his inherited predilection for all forms of outdoor sport and manly exercise and taught him the value of hard physical training. At one time he is beating the jungle for deer or hawking for pheasants,—even when his hand was injured, he was able to bring down a flying buck with an arrow at long range: at another he is hunting the rhinoceros near Peshawar: again, he speaks of a chase after a wild ass:—"Spurring forward and getting into position quite close to it, I chopped at the nape of its neck behind the ears and cut through the wind-pipe; it stopped, rolled over and died. My sword cut well! The wild ass was surprisingly fat." Swimming and bathing were also favourite pastimes: he made a point of swimming every river that he met on his wanderings, including the Ganges, which, as he writes, he crossed with thirty-three strokes and then re-crossed in the same way without a rest. He thought nothing of plunging into an ice-bound stream, with the temperature well below zero: and one of his solaces in India was bathing. "Three things oppressed us (in India)—the heat, the violent winds, the dust. Against all three the bath is a protection, for in it, what is known of dust and winds? And in the heat it is so chilly that one is almost cold." If cleanliness is next to godliness, Babur certainly prepared for himself a path to sainthood.

With the *penchant* for travel and excursion, which was ingrained in the Mongol of the steppes, he combined an educated taste for sight-seeing and investigation. Some one tells him of a tomb at Ghazni, which moved when a benediction on the Prophet was pronounced over it. He sets out at once to investigate the phenomenon, and discovers that "the movement was a trick, presumably of the tomb-attendants, who had built a sort of platform above it, which moved when pushed, so that to those upon it the tomb seemed to move, just as the shore does to those passing in a boat." Deceit and quackery of any kind were hateful to Babur, who promptly ordered the demolition of the platform and the immediate discontinuance of the imposture. The extent to which travel of one kind or another filled his life may be gauged from his own statement, that from the age of eleven he never observed the Feast of Ramzan for two years running in the same place. And while these peregrinations were often forced upon him by political misfortune or by the exigencies of warfare, they taught him his road-craft and topography, and how to guide his course by the face of Nature. Mark him as he rides forth one pitch-dark night against the Ghilji Afghans. Not a man can be found to show the road. "In the end," he adds, "I took the lead. I had been in those parts several times before; drawing inferences from those days, I took the Pole-star on my right shoulder-blade and with some anxiety moved on. God brought it right!" It was from Babur and their more remote nomad ancestors that Akbar and his successors inherited their love of camping-expeditions. Jahangir, "the royal stroller *par excellence*," was devoted to excursions; Shah Jahan sought recreation in marching by slow stages to Kashmir. Yet how different from Babur's wanderings were the style and circumstances of their expeditions, furnished and supported by the immense wealth of an imperial exchequer! The emperor no longer galloped at the head of a column of braves, with the Pole-star on his shoulder-blade, but was borne upon a richly-caparisoned elephant amid all the luxury and paraphernalia of a vast moving city; while at night, in front of his purple pavilion, a giant beacon signalled the sovereign will that moved the tumultuous mass of functionaries, slaves, eunuchs, and the whole retinue of the imperial harem.

A sterling feature of Babur's personality was his loyalty to kinsmen and friends and to his plighted word. Infidelity he deemed the most odious of crimes, and he could scarcely find words to express his disgust and horror, when Khushrau Shah blinded one of his benefactor's sons and murdered another. "A hundred thousand curses," he writes, "light on him who planned and did a deed so horrible! Up to the very verge of Resurrection let him who hears of this act of Khushrau Shah curse him; and may he who, hearing, curses not, know cursing equally deserved!" The crime was aggravated in Babur's eyes by the fact that Khushrau Shah, though possessed of wide territories and hosts of armed retainers, "had not the pluck to stand up to a hen!" When Muhammad Dost was caught and blinded by the Uzbegs as a punishment for treachery, Babur found ample justification for their action in the popular adage "the salt took his eyes." No punishment was too severe for infidelity.

On the other hand, the misdeeds or shortcomings of his own family never affected Babur's loyalty towards them. He treated his distant Chaghatai kinsmen with a generosity and consideration, which at times were ill-requited: he was equally loyal to his Timurid relations. Qambar Ali once urged him to desert the Mughal Khans and join Tambal against them. "Would that be right?" he replied: "the Khans are my blood-relations: better serve them than rule for Tambal." During his march to Kabul, Bāqi Beg advised Babur to get rid of his brother, Jahangir, by sending him to Khurasan. But, "urge it as he would, I did not accept his suggestion, because it is against my nature to do an injury to my brethren, older or younger, or to any kinsman soever, even when something untoward has happened." Again, when his other brother, Nasir Mirza, was attacked and stripped of all his possessions by the Begs of Badakshan, Babur, forgiving and forgetting his earlier misbehaviour, welcomed him warmly at Kabul and sought by generous treatment to restore his peace of mind. To his friends and their memory he was ever faithful. One of the oldest, Mir Khwaja Kalan, is mentioned affectionately in a letter written by Babur in India to Humayun at Kabul; another, Nuyan Kukuldash, came to an untimely end soon after Babur's first conquest of Samarkand. Twenty-five years afterwards Babur recalls the story that one Munim, whom he styles "that sodomite," had taken Nuyan's life. Yet "none knew the truth. His death made me strangely sad: for few men have I felt such grief. I wept unceasingly for a week or ten days. The chronogram of his death was found in the words *Nuyan is dead*." This was the emperor's *ave atque vale* to one whom he loved as a brother.

In matters of honour Babur was as punctilious as he was loyal. When Shaikh Bayazid invited him secretly to Akhsi in 1502-03, in the hope of separating him from his uncles the Khans, he informed them at once of the intrigue. They urged him to go to Akhsi in response to the overture, and by fair or foul means take the Shaikh prisoner. Babur flatly refused. "It was not my habit to cheat and play false," he explains; "Here above all places, when promises would have been made, how was I to break them?" At a subsequent conference with Bayazid he was again pressed to seize him and his comrades, and again he refused, saying "matters are past making prisoners." Even in the case of Khushrau Shah, whom he loathed more than all men for his vicious and treacherous habits, he adhered strictly to his pledged word. In 1504-05 Khushrau Shah, who had fallen on evil days, approached Babur as a suppliant. Mirza Khan demanded that he should be put to death as a punishment for his dastardly assassination of the Mirza's brethren. "Many of us," says Babur, "were at one with him, for truly it it right both by law and common justice that such men should get their deserts. But, as terms had been made, Khushrau Shah was allowed to go free." Such incidents as these prove the value of the training given to him in early years by the Mongol women of his family. The failings of the Turki character, if indeed

Babur inherited them, had yielded to the simple honesty of the pastoral nomad.

According to Babur, an honourable reputation was more to be desired than fine gold, and his open admiration of good character was only equalled by his contempt for those who flouted the world's approbation. "If a man have any share of intelligence," he wrote in allusion to the cowardice of one Kupuk Mirza, "why try to be ill-spoken of after death? If he be ambitious, why not try so to act that men will praise him, when gone? In the honourable mention of their names, wise men find a second life!" His character-sketches of his contemporaries testify to his appreciation of human worth and virtue. Of one he remarks—"He was a pious God-fearing Musalman, an abstainer from doubtful aliments, excellent in judgment and counsel;" another is "an excellent soldier; my father before me had favoured him, making him keeper of the Seal; he was a student of theology, had great acquaintance with words and good style; moreover he understood hawking and rain-making with the jade-stone." Of yet another he writes, "When the enemy, after taking possession of Andijan, heard of my arrival in Khujand, they martyred Khwaja-i-Maulana-i-qazi by hanging him with dishonour in the Gate of the Citadel. . . . I have no doubt he was a Saint; what better witness to his sanctity than the fact, that within a short time no sign or trace remained of those active for his death? He was a wonderful man: it was not in him to be afraid; in no other man was seen such courage as his. This quality is a further witness to his sanctity. Other men, however bold, have anxieties and tremors; he had none."

Among other salient features of Babur's character were his hatred of meanness in any form and his open contempt for wealth and money. The following censure was passed by him upon Baqi Chaghaniani, who for some time was associated with Babur's fortunes and actually placed his family under Babur's protection:—

> "So miserly was he that, although when we left Tirmiz with his family and possessions, he may have owned 30 to 40

> thousand sheep, and although these masses of sheep used to pass in front of us at every camping-ground, he did not give a single one to our bare braves, tortured as they were by the pangs of hunger; at last in Kahmard he gave 50! "

Subsequently he became so disgusted with Baqi that he granted him permission to depart, and shortly afterwards the miser was robbed and killed by highway thieves.

> " We ourselves had let Baqi go without injuring him, but his own misdeeds rose up against him, his own acts defeated him.
>
> Leave thou to Fate the man who does thee wrong ;
> For Fate is an avenging servitor."

Babur himself was singularly free from the *auri sacra fames*. When in 1507-08 his brother Nasir Mirza unauthorisedly seized the contents of the Kandahar treasury, which had been loaded on camels for despatch to Kabul, Babur never demanded their restoration. " I just gave them to him" is his laconic statement. One can imagine the shock to his feelings when he learnt that Humayun, his much-loved son, had acted in the same way at Delhi, seizing without permission several treasuries. "It grieved me sorely," he admits: "I wrote and despatched to him very severe reproaches." Babur's refusal to accept the famous *Koh-i-Nur* diamond is perhaps the clearest illustration of his freedom from avarice. When Humayun reached Agra after the battle of Panipat, he placed a guard upon the family of Raja Bikramajit of Gwalior, who had fallen on the battlefield. In return for their freedom, the captives offered Humayun a large store of jewels and valuables, including the famous diamond, the value of which, according to Babur, was deemed equivalent to the cost of two and a half days' food for the whole world. He then adds, "Humayun offered it to me when I arrived in Agra. I just gave it back to him." It is doubtful whether any other potentate of that age would have displayed the same indifference to so priceless a gem: it is certain that any one of his wealthy successors—Akbar, Jahangir, or Shah Jahan—would have taken immediate steps to secure it for himself. In his attitude towards worldly wealth, Babur stands alone among the Great Mughals.

In social matters he was a stickler for etiquette, and was intolerant of breaches of good manners and decorum. An Afghan visitor, who demanded unusual precedence, was soon put in his place. "These Afghans remain very boorish and tactless! This person asked to sit, although Dilawar Khan, his superior in following and in rank, was not seated, and although the sons of Alam Khan, who are of royal birth, did not sit. Little ear was lent to his unreason." For the same reason he demanded from others the respect due to his own birth and position. When on his second visit to Badiuz-zaman Mirza he was treated with less courtesy than on a previous occasion, he made a dignified protest, reminding the host and his nobles that "small though my age was (24 years), my place of honour was large; that I had seated myself twice on the throne of our forefathers in Samarkand by blow straight-dealt, and that to be laggard in showing me respect was unreasonable, since it was for this (Timurid) dynasty's sake I had thus fought and striven with that alien foe." His words went home; the Mirza admitted his error. Even in his lighter moments amid the wine-cups he stood by the same principle; he drank his wine like a gentleman and expected others to follow his lead; ribald behaviour distressed him and generally ended in the exclusion of the offender.

Though he had much to try his patience and his temper, Babur rarely gave way to passion. Once, it is true, when an equerry brought him a worthless horse to ride, he gave the man such a blow in the face that he sprained his own wrist: but, as a rule, mistakes and disaster merely served as a stimulus to his indomitable geniality. Think for a moment of his escape from Samarkand, the home of his fathers, the goal of his dreams. It is midnight. Accompanied by a few followers, by his loyal and courageous mother and two other women, he rides into the darkness—a homeless fugitive. At this crisis of his fortunes, if ever, he had cause for dejection and self-pity. But that was not Babur's way. Scarcely out of arrow-shot of the walls, he starts racing with two of his men.

> "My horse was leading, when I, thinking to look at theirs behind, twisted myself round; the girth may have slackened, for my saddle turned and I was thrown on my head on the ground. Although I at once got up and remounted, my brain did not steady till the evening. Till then this world and what went on appeared to me like things felt and seen in a dream or fancy."

Even a severe concussion could not rob Babur of his spirits and appetite. At their first halt he and his party killed and roasted a horse, and after making a square meal off it, rode forward to safety in Dizak.

This light-heartedness in adversity was partly responsible for Babur's influence over other men. His unruffled equanimity gave him a superiority which they readily acknowledged, and lent to his words of promise or exhortation an authority which would have been denied to the advice of a leader of less resilient spirit. There is no finer episode in Babur's career than his address to his chiefs and men before the critical struggle with Rana Sanga. Reports of the great strength and prowess of the Rajput chivalry had been freely bruited abroad: alarm was spreading in Babur's camp: panic and desertion were imminent. The action which he took at this crisis is best described in his own terse phrases:—

> "At length after I had made enquiry concerning people's want of heart and had seen their slackness for myself, a plan occurred to me. I summoned all the Begs and braves, and said to them:—'Begs and braves!
>
> 'Who comes into the world will die;
> What lasts and lives will be God.
> He who hath entered the assembly of life,
> Drinketh at last of the cup of death.
> He who hath come to the rim of life,
> Passeth at last from earth's house of woe.
> Better than life with a bad name, is death with a good one.
> Well is it with me, if I die with a good name!
> A good name must I have, since the body is death's.

God the Most High has allotted to us such happiness and has created for us such good fortune that we die as martyrs, we kill as avengers of His cause. Therefore must each of you take oath upon His Holy Word that he will not think of turning his face from this foe, or withdraw from this deadly encounter, so long as life is not rent from his body.' All those present, Beg and retainer, great and small, took the Holy Book joyfully into their hands and made vow and compact to this purport. The plan was perfect; it worked admirably for those near and afar, for seërs and hearers, for friend and foe."

The speech incidentally reveals the chief bulwark of Babur's manhood, namely, his abiding faith in the assistance and power of the Creator. To this belief may be traced the serenity and fortitude which he displayed throughout the trials and chances of a chequered life. As a child he must have received a good grounding in the Koran and the precepts of Islam, and was taught to observe strictly the rules of daily life prescribed for the orthodox Musalman. "This year," he remarks in his diary for 1494, "I began to abstain from all doubtful food; my obedience extended even to the knife, the spoon, and the tablecloth. Also the after-midnight prayer was less neglected." When he succumbed to the lure of the wine-cup, he never forgot that he was breaking one of the articles of his Faith, and in his later repentance he described the lapse as a sin which "had set a lasting stain upon my heart." The sincerity of his self-accusation is proved by his strict adherence to the vow of total abstinence, which he took before the battle of Kanwaha.

True Musalman as he was, he found no room in his creed for religious tolerance. Nurtured in the orthodox tenets of the Sunni sect, he regarded other forms of belief with contempt and aversion. In his eyes the Shias were "rank heretics," followers of "an evil belief opposed to the pure Faith;" while the Hindus were "Pagans," against whom it was almost his bounden duty to wage a Holy War. This term he applies to his struggle with Rana Sanga, and by virtue of his victory over the Hindu chieftain he assumes the title of *Ghazi* or "victor in a Holy War." The capture of Chanderi, which gave the *coup-de-grâce* to Hindu militant opposition, was celebrated by "a pillar of pagan heads set up on a hill." He was no less severe, according to his own statement, on the people of Bajaur.

> "As the Bajauris were rebels and at enmity with the people of Islam, and as by reason of the heathenish and hostile customs prevailing in their midst, the very name of Islam was rooted out from their tribe, they were put to general massacre and their wives and children were made captive. At a guess more than 3,000 men went to their death."

The symbols and structures of other religions and beliefs were equally obnoxious to him, and his treatment of the tomb of a heretic qalandar, who had "perverted a body of Yusufzai," was identical with that accorded to two Jain statues at Urwa. In both cases he ordered their destruction. It is in his treatment of those whom he had been taught to regard as schismatics or idolaters that we catch a glimpse of the ruthlessness to be expected of a descendant of Timur and Chenghiz Khan, and his slaughter of the infidel Bajauris, though consonant with the teaching of militant Islam, may be regarded as a momentary reversion to Central Asian savagery. At the same time he never indulged in prolonged persecutions or pogroms, nor did he allow individuals to suffer punishment solely on the grounds of religious dogma. Despite his rooted antipathy to those who were not orthodox Sunnis, his usually genial nature would probably have revolted against such atrocities as the Inquisition, the St. Bartholomew massacres, or the Dragonnades of Christian Europe.

As regards his personal religion, he cherished a firm belief in the guidance and intervention of Allah. He ascribed all his successes to God's favour, all his disasters to God's inscrutable will. When, after his father's death, Sultan Ahmad Mirza's design of conquering Farghana was frustrated by a series of unforeseen obstacles, Babur declared that "The Almighty God, who of his perfect power and without mortal aid has ever brought my affairs to their right issue, made such things happen here that they became disgusted at having advanced and turned back with nothing done." It was "by God's grace" that he recovered Andijan after two years' exile; by "the favour and mercy of the most High God" that he won his first pitched battle; it was the same "Almighty Power" which placed Kabul and Ghazni in his hands. In describing the attack on the Kabul rebels in 1507, when an adversary brought his sword down on Babur's unprotected arm, he ascribes his escape from injury to a prayer which he had previously offered, and adds, "only by God's grace can it have been that not a hairbreadth of harm was done to me;

> If a sword shook the Earth from her place,
> Not a vein would it cut till God wills."

Babur's reliance upon a Higher Power and his conviction that all issues are fore-ordained by God, manifest themselves in all the more important events of his career. A phrase in the earlier pages of his *Memoirs*,—"We put our trust in God and made another expedition to

Samarkand"—finds its counterpart in a later entry,—"I put my foot in the stirrup of resolution and my hand on the rein of trust in God, and moved forward against Sultan Ibrahim." It was God to whom he looked for a safe issue of the perilous mountain journey from Khurasan to Kabul in 1506-07, and on whom he expressly relied for victory at Kandahar.

> "Without a glance at the fewness of our men, we had the nagarets sounded, and putting our trust in God moved with face set for Muqim (his opponent).
>
> For few or for many God is full strength,
> No man has might in His Court.
>
> How often, God willing it, a small force has vanquished a large one! Learning from the nagarets that we were approaching, Muqim forget his fixed plan and took the road of flight. God brought it right!"

The fears which obsessed his men before they joined issue with Ibrahim Lodi's forces at Panipat, called forth the reproof,—"Nothing recommends anxiety and fear. For why? because what God has fixed in eternity cannot be changed." Once again, before Chanderi, when Khalifa in a panic brought him news of the defeat of his eastern expeditionary force, Babur answered calmly,—"There is no ground for perturbation or alarm: nothing comes to pass but what is pre-destined of God. As this task (the siege of Chanderi) is ahead of us, not a breath must be drawn about what we have heard. To-morrow we will assault the fort: that done, we shall see what comes." And once more, to use his constant phrase, "God brought it right!"

Babur was strongly convinced of the efficacy of prayer— not merely the performance of the five daily services enjoined upon all the Faithful, but personal supplication, which is recommended, though not imperatively demanded, by the law of the Prophet. In the course of his narrative he mentions three grave occasions on which he interceded personally with God,— once, when he prayed for the souls of his mother, his grandmother, and the younger Khan, all of whom died about the same time; again, when he prayed in the garden at Kabul for a sign that his invasion of India would be successful; and a third time when he besought the Almighty to protect him in his struggle with the Kabul rebels. As has already been mentioned, he escaped a severe sword-wound in an almost miraculous manner, and attributed his immunity to the special prayer which he had offered in these words :—

> "O my God! Thou art my Creator. Except Thee there is no God. On Thee do I repose my trust. Thou art the Lord of the mighty throne. What Gods wills comes to pass, and what he does not will, will not come to pass : and there is no power or strength save through the high and exalted God. And of a truth, in all things God is Almighty; and verily he comprehends all things by his knowledge, and has taken account of everything. O my Creator! as I sincerely trust in Thee, do Thou seize by the forelock all evil proceeding from within myself, and all evil coming from without, and all evil

> proceeding from every man who can be the occasion of evil, and all such evil as can proceed from any living thing, and remove them far from me. Since, of a truth, Thou art the Lord of the exalted throne."

There was one more occasion in Babur's life, not recorded in his own *Memoirs*, but vouched for by others, when he had recourse to prayer for deliverance from overwhelming anxiety. Humayun lay sick unto death, and, as will be described in a later page, the emperor prayed with all his soul and strength for his son's deliverance. The fulfilment of his prayer was the last boon vouchsafed to him by the Deity, to whom through all the turmoil of his active life, and notwithstanding the transgression for a season of the religious prohibition of wine, he had shown the unquestioning obedience and reverence of a true Believer.

CHAPTER II

THE DAY OF ADVERSITY

" *Quidquid erit, superanda omnis fortuna ferendo est.*"

Ascending the throne of Farghana at the age of eleven, Babur had experienced every caprice of Fortune ere he reached his twentieth year. At one time the ruler of subject provinces, at another the victim of his own ambitious and disloyal nobles, he had been accorded the honours of a conqueror and had tasted the bitterness of exile amid the inhospitable mountains of Transoxiana. In his narrative of the vicissitudes and dangers through which he won his way to fame, one can mark the gradual moulding of his finely-tempered spirit. The troubles of his early years, as was perhaps natural, caused him some bitterness and depression; he confesses that he "could not help crying a good deal," when he failed to secure help in recovering Andijan in 1497-98, and when all his men, save two or three hundred loyal souls, deserted his cause. His feelings were greatly wounded in 1500-01 by the lack of courtesy shown to him by the despicable Khusrau Shah, controller of Hisar and Kunduz, who treated him with less respect than the lowest servant. Babur salved his heart, as he usually did in moments of distress and sorrow, by resort to poetry, and wrote the following *extempore* couplet on Khusrau's shortcomings:—

> Who, o my heart! has seen goodness from worldings?
> Look not for goodness from him who has none.

In May, 1501, he confronted Shaibani Beg at Sar-i-pul, and was forced to retire into Samarkand. The retreat became a *sauve qui peut.*

> "Ten or fifteen men were left with me. The Kohik water was close by. We rode straight for it. It was the season when it comes down in flood. We rode right into it, man and horse in mail. It was just fordable for half-way over; after that it

> had to be swum. For more than an arrow's flight (about 400 yards) we, man and mount in mail! made our horses swim and so got across. Once out of the water, we cut off the horse armour and let it lie."

This unfortunate defeat was followed by the siege of Samarkand, which lasted for six months and ended in Babur's capitulation. He and his followers suffered great privations; the people were forced to eat the flesh of dogs and asses, and to feed their horses on wood-shavings and the leaves of mulberry and elm. The disaster impressed upon Babur the truth of the maxim that the fallen have no friends, and that for assistance in adversity he must rely mainly upon himself. He invoked help from all sides; but "no one helped or reinforced me when I was in strength and power, and had suffered no sort of defeat or loss; on what score would anyone help me now?" He embodies the lesson of his misfortune in a verse, written later at Tashkend:—

> Except my soul, no friend worth trust found I,
> Except my heart, no confidant found I.

Thus expelled from Samarkand, Babur wandered homeless with a few followers in the hills of Farghana, and eventually decided to take refuge with his uncles, the Khans, at Tashkend in June, 1502. He was almost at the end of his tether, when he decided to seek their hospitality; only his indomitable pluck brought him safely through the ordeal. But the references in the *Memoirs* to his circumstances at this juncture show how greatly his pride must have suffered from "the slings and arrows of outrageous Fortune."

> "During my stay in Tashkend I endured much poverty and humiliation. No country or hope of one! Most of my retainers dispersed; those left, unable to move about with me because of their destitution! . . . . This uncertainty and want of house and home drove me at last to despair. Said I, 'It would be better to take my head (a rider's metaphor) and go away than live in such misery; better to go as far as my feet can carry me than be seen of men in such poverty and humiliation.'

> Having settled to go to China, I resolved to take my head and get away. From my childhood I had wished to visit China, but had not been able to manage it because of ruling and attachments. Now sovereignty itself was gone! and my mother, for her part, was re-united to her mother and her younger brother. The hindrance to my journey had been removed: my anxiety for my mother was dispelled."

Fate decreed that Babur should not see the Celestial Kingdom, and China's loss ultimately proved India's gain. The arrival of the younger Khan at Tashkend put an end to his plans, and by July, 1502, the two uncles had helped him to recover the greater portion of his hereditary kingdom.

But the cup of Babur's affliction was not yet full. In June, 1503 the Khans were defeated at Akhsi by that militant barbarian, Shaibani or Shaibaq Khan, and Babur, who had already been ousted from Farghana by his old enemy, Sultan Ahmad Tambal, was driven once more into exile amid the mountains of Sukh and Hushiar.

The desperate straits to which he was reduced—he escaped with only one follower—can be gauged from the narrative of his flight from Tambal's army.

> "Our horses could not possibly gallop, they trotted. His began to flag. Said I, 'What will become of me if you fall behind? Come along! Let us live or die together.' Several times I looked back at him; at last he cried, 'My horse is done! It cannot go on. Never mind me! You go on, perhaps you will get away.' It was a miserable position for me; he remained behind, I was alone."

Soon afterwards he was joined by a few more of his followers with their families, and by his mother, who remained loyally by his side during these months of hardship, when his fortunes were at their lowest ebb. The little band of homeless fugitives, surrounded by enemies, passed about twelve months in the hills in great poverty, owing their survival solely to the loyalty or compassion of the wild nomads of that region. "At length," in the words of Mrs. Beveridge, "the ragged and destitute company had to move, and started in mid-June, 1504, on that perilous mountain journey, to which Haidar applies the Prophet's words, "Travel is a foretaste of Hell," but of which the end was the establishment of a Timurid dynasty in Hindustan."

Babur's courage and vitality were never more conspicuous than at this crisis of his fortunes. He was not yet 22 years of age, when he determined to bid farewell to the beloved country of his birth and to carve out a new future for himself and his kinsfolk in Kabul, which had been seized by the Arghun Mongols after the death of his uncle, Ulugh Beg Mirza, King of Kabul, in 1501. In Farghana he had been the unwilling victim of older men's ambitious intrigues; his boyhood had been overshadowed by wholly undeserved hostility. But although he had thereby been deprived of his heritage, he had acquired amid failure, privation and danger a far more precious possession—a heart schooled to meet adversity with a smile and to value more than fine gold the kindness and fidelity of others. It was a sorry little band of pilgrims that set out upon the long march across the hills to Afghanistan.

> "Those who went with me into exile, hoping in me, were, small and great, between 200 and 300. They were almost all on foot, had walking staves in their hands, brogues (rough boots of untanned leather) on their feet, and long coats on their shoulders. So destitute were we that we had but two tents among us; my own used to be pitched for my mother, and they set an *alachuq* (a felt covering with flexible poles) at each stage for me to sit in."

In this wise Babur, founder of the Mughal Empire of India, left the home of his forefathers for ever.

Had he not been endowed with singular vigour and powers of endurance, Babur could not have survived the trials of his early years. In proof of his physical strength, Erskine recalls the fact that he used to leap from pinnacle to pinnacle of the ramparts in his double-soled boots, and often performed this feat while carrying a man under each arm. His *Memoirs* afford many other instances of his bodily powers. In 1498, while ill with high fever, he rode between 70 and 80 miles to attack the fortified town of Rabat-i-Khwaja: on another occasion he rode more than 148 miles with only the briefest halts: he thought nothing of galloping about 48 miles from Marghinan to Andijan between sunrise and noon. Even three years of continuous work in the hot plains of Hindustan, marked by intermittent attacks of fever, failed to reduce his power of sustained physical effort; for he tells us that in June, 1529—the hottest season of the Indian year—he rode 157 miles from Adampur to Agra between midnight on a Tuesday and 9 p.m. on Thursday. He always kept himself in hard training; he swam every river that he met on his wanderings; and during his sojourn in the mountainous tracts of Samarkand he made constant excursions barefooted, and, to quote his own words, "from doing this so much, my feet became so that rock and stone made no difference to them."

It was perhaps in the deadly cold of the winter months to the north of the Oxus that his endurance was most conspicuous. Once when he and his men rode all night to Akhsi, the cold was so intense that several of them had their hands, feet and ears frostbitten. Of another expedition he writes:—

> "So cold it was that during the two or three days we were in those parts, several men died of it. Needing to make ablution, I went into an irrigation channel, frozen along both banks, but because of its swift current not ice-bound in the middle, and I bathed, dipping under sixteen times. The cold of the water went quite through me."

He suffered great hardship during the passage of the Sara-Taq Pass with its "ravines, precipices, perilous heights and knife-edge saddles;" but his worst journey was taken over the Zirrin Pass in the teeth of a heavy snowstorm—a Pass that "no long-memoried elder" had ever heard of any attempt to cross in such weather, or indeed of any suggestion of crossing at that time of the year. On Babur's own admission the miseries of that journey surpassed all his previous experiences; yet, in accordance with his usual habit, he turned in his distress to poetry and partially relieved his discomfort by composing the following couplet:—

> Is there one cruel turn of Fortune's wheel unseen of me?
> Is there a pang, a grief my wounded heart has missed?

Of his bravery in battle it is needless to speak at length. He fought as one would have expected him to fight, owing his victory or safety on more than one occasion to his hard physical condition. In the Mughal rebellion of 1508-09 he defeated five champions of his adversaries in single combat: as a boy of 19 he captured Samarkand at the head of only 240 men—an achievement comparable with Timur's capture of Qarchi and certainly more creditable than Sultan Husain Mirza's capture of Herat in 1470. His courage in the face of heavy odds is well illustrated by the tale of his first attempt upon Andijan in 1502.

"Suddenly about the third watch, there rose a war-cry and a sound of drums. Sleepy and startled, ignorant whether the foe was many or few, my men, without looking to one another, took each his own road and turned for flight. There was no time for me to get at them: I went straight for the enemy. Only Mir Shah Quchin and Baba Sherzad and Nasir Dost sprang forward. We four excepted, every man set his face for flight. I had gone a little way forward, when the enemy rode rapidly up, flung out his war-cry, and poured arrows on us. One man, on a horse with a starred forehead, came close to me: I shot at it; it rolled over and died. They made a little as if to retire. The three with me said, 'In this darkness it is not certain whether they are many or few; all our men have gone off; what harm can we four do them? Fighting must be when we have overtaken our runaways and rallied them. . .' Off we hurried, got up with our men, and beat and horsewhipped some of them; but, do what we would, they would not make a stand. Back the four of us went to shoot arrows at the foe. They drew a little back, but when, after a discharge or two, they saw we were not more than three or four, they busied themselves in chasing and unhorsing my men. I went three or four times to try and rally my men, but all in vain! They were not to be brought to order. Back I went with my three and kept the foe in check with our arrows. They pursued us two to three *kuroh* (4-6 miles) as far as the rising ground opposite Kharabuk and Pashamun. There we met Muhammad Ali Mubashir. Said I, 'They are only a few; let us stop and put our horses at them.' So we did. When we got up to them, they stood still."

At Andijan again in the following year he was shot through the right leg with an arrow, and, thus wounded, was attacked by Sultan Ahmad Tambal himself. "I had on the cap of my helm. Tambal chopped so violently at my head that it lost all feeling under the blow.

A large wound was made in my head, though not a thread of the cap was cut. I had not bared my sword; it was in the scabbard; and I had no chance to draw it. Single-handed I was alone among many foes." Nevertheless he fought his way to safety and recovered rapidly from his wounds. We catch a characteristic glimpse of him again in the forefront of the battle against the Hazaras in 1505-06. "As we had gone forward in haste, most of us were not in mail. Shaft after shaft flew by and fell: with each one Ahmad said anxiously, 'Bare like this you go into it! I have seen two arrows go close to your head!' Said I, 'Fear not! many as good arrows as these have flown past my head!'"

Babur's methods of warfare were generally in keeping with those of the wild Turks, Mongols and Uzbegs among whom he was brought up. He speaks with approval of Sultan Husain Mirza's practice of beheading his prisoners, and he himself followed the Mongol custom of erecting pyramids of the heads of those slain or taken captive in battle. During his first expedition to India one of his camps was marked by three minarets of Afghan skulls, and a few days later he recounts how "forty or fifty Afghans, falling to the arrow, falling to the sword, were cut to pieces. After making a clean sweep of them, we dismounted in a field of growing corn and ordered a tower of their heads to be set up." A similar trophy of "pagan heads" was erected after his defeat of Rana Sanga and the Hindu confederacy at Kanwaha; and it seems probable that from this savage feature of Mongol warfare were borrowed the *chor-minars* or masonry pillars, studded with the heads of thieves and robbers, which were so often observed by travellers on the outskirts of Indian towns in Shah Jahan's reign.

Babur's military discipline was severe and his punishments, according to modern standards, were often cruel. While on the march through Bhira, he issued the following order to his troops, "Do no hurt or harm to the flocks and herds of these people, not even to their cotton-ends and broken needles;" and on receipt of a report that some of his men had neglected the order and had harassed the people, he gave instant orders for some of the delinquents to be executed and others to have their noses slit and be led in disgrace round the camp. "Khusrau Shah's people," he writes on another occasion, "were well practised in oppression and violence. They tyrannised over one after another, till at last I had up one of Sayyidim Ali's good braves to my Gate (i.e. outside Babur's tent, where justice was administered) and there beaten for forcibly taking a jar of oil. There and then he just died under the blows. His example kept the rest down." He dispensed the same rough and ready justice to several of his men, who had attacked and wounded the attendants at the tomb of a Pir. Upon slackness, cowardice, or treachery, especially when camped in an enemy's country, he was justifiably severe. During his halts in the Isa Khel country, he shared with his chief officers the duty of making the rounds of the camp every night, and any man found absent from his post was at once sentenced to have his nose slit and be led round the ranks in disgrace. He deprived of their rank and station certain of his Begs, who had sat supine and idle, while one of Babur's stoutest fighters was engaged single-handed and slain by a body of Afghans. Such cowards, he declared, ought to have their beards shaved and be publicly exhibited. When, on the road from Ghazni to Khelat, he was informed that Sher Ali and others were planning desertion, he had them all arrested; and as this was by no means Sher Ali's first offence, he was straightway put to death. The others he dismissed with the loss of their horses and arms.

Despotism has always demanded and countenanced swift and savage punishment in cases of attempt upon the life of the ruler. When one remembers the fate of Damiens, who attempted the life of Louis XV in 1757—the bed of steel, the prolonged torture, the dismemberment by wild horses—one can hardly blame Babur overmuch for his sentence upon those who sought to poison him in December, 1526. The crime was particularly despicable, as the chief conspirator, mother of his vanquished foe Ibrahim Lodi, had been treated by Babur with great deference and consideration. Here is the episode in his own words:—

> "The ill-omened old woman, Ibrahim's mother, heard that I ate things from the

hands of Hindustanis—the fact being that three or four months earlier, as I had not seen Hindustani dishes, I had ordered Ibrahim's cooks to be brought, and out of 50 or 60 had kept four. Of this she heard, sent to Etawa for Ahmad the *chashnigir*—in Hindustan they call a taster a *chashnigir*—and having got him, gave a *tula* of poison, wrapped in a square of paper, into the hand of a slave-woman, who was to give it to him. That poison Ahmad gave to the Hindustani cooks in the kitchen, promising them four *parganas* if they would somehow get it into the food. Following the first slave-woman, that ill-omened old woman sent a second to see if the first did or did not give the poison she had received to Ahmad. Well was it that Ahmad put the poison, not into the cooking-pot, but on a dish. He did not put it into the pot, because I had strictly ordered the tasters to compel any Hindustanis who were present while food was cooking in the pots, to taste the food. Our graceless tasters were neglectful when the food was being dished up. Thin slices of bread were put on a porcelain dish: on these less than half of the packet of poison was sprinkled, and over this buttered fritters were laid. It would have been bad if the poison had been strewn on the fritters or thrown into the pot. In his confusion the man threw the larger half into the fire-place.

"On Friday late after the Afternoon Prayer, when the cooked meats were set out, I ate a good deal of a dish of hare and also much fried carrot, took a few mouthfuls of the poisoned Hindustani food without noticing any unpleasant flavour, took also a mouthful or two of dried meat. Then I felt sick. As some dried meat eaten on the previous day had had an unpleasant taste, I thought my nausea due to the dried meat. Again and again my heart rose; after retching two or three times I was near vomiting on the tablecloth. At last I saw it would not do, got up, went retching every moment of the way to the closet and on reaching it vomited much.

Never had I vomited after food, used not to do so indeed after drinking. I became suspicious: I had the cooks put in ward and ordered some of the vomit to be given to a dog, and the dog to be watched. It was somewhat out of sorts near the first watch of the next day; its belly was swollen, and however much people threw stones at it and turned it over, it did not get up; in that state it remained till mid-day; it then got up; it did not die. One or two of the braves, who also had eaten of that dish, vomited a good deal next day; one was in a very bad state. In the end all escaped. '*An evil arrived but happily passed.*' God gave me new birth! I am coming from that other world; I am born to-day of my mother: I was sick; I live; through God, I know to-day the worth of life!

"I ordered Paymaster Sultan Muhammad to watch the cook. When he was taken for torture, he related the above particulars one after another.

Monday being Court day, I ordered the grandees and notables, amirs and wazirs to be present, and that those two men and two women should be brought and questioned. They there related the particulars of the affair. That taster I had cut in pieces, that cook skinned alive; one of those women I had thrown under an elephant, the other shot with a matchlock. The old woman I had kept under guard; she will meet her doom, the captive of her own act" [she threw herself into the Indus and was drowned].

Except in such circumstances as those above-mentioned, which involved the maintenance of discipline or the stern discouragement of treason, Babur frequently displayed a clemency towards prisoners and others, which was strikingly at variance with the attitude of some of his predecessors and contemporaries. He was always ready to listen to representations and entreaties on behalf of those condemned to death, as for example, when he released four men at the request of Kasim Beg in 1509, and fifteen Hazara thieves whom he had determined to put to death by torture, "as a warning to all highwaymen and robbers." During his first campaign in India he performed many acts of mercy; and such barbarities as were perpetrated were generally the work of Khusrau Shah's undisciplined caterans or of the independent Begs who had for the time being joined his standard, and over whom he exercised no real control. Towards non-combatants and the general public he appears to have acted with great consideration. At Yam, for example, in 1497 his troops ruthlessly plundered the Muhammadan traders of the town; yet, "such was the discipline of our army that, an order to restore everything having been given, the first watch of the next day had not passed, before nothing, not a tag of cotton, not a broken needle's point, remained in the possession of any man of the force. All was back with its owners." Again, when he entered Khelat in 1507-08, he found a large body of Indian merchants who had come there for trade. "The general opinion about them," writes Babur, "was that people who at a time of such hostilities come into an enemy's country, must be plundered. With this, however, I did not agree. Said I, 'What is the traders' offence? If we, looking to God's pleasure, leave such scrapings of gain aside, the Most High God will apportion our reward.'" One can well imagine that this broad-minded and merciful attitude, which redounds to Babur's credit, would not have found favour with his ancestors Chinghiz Khan and Timur, to whom the lives and property of other men were of absolutely no account.

His inclination to show compassion to transgressors extended even to those guilty of active disloyalty—an offence which most Muhammadan potentates would have punished with swift and cruel death. The *Memoirs* enable us to witness the scene when Mirza Khan, the leader of the Kabul rebellion, was hailed before Babur by his guards.

> "Said I to him, 'Come, let's have a look at one another'; but twice before he could bend the knee and come forward, he fell down through agitation. When we had looked at one another, I placed him by my side to give him heart, and I drank first of

> the sherbet brought in, in order to remove his fears. As those who had joined him, soldiers, peasants, Mughals and Chaghatais were in suspense, we simply ordered him to remain for a few days in his elder sister's house. A few days later he was allowed to leave for Khurasan."

His treatment of the aged traitor, Daulat Khan Lodi, was equally magnanimous. Addressing his prisoner, Babur said :—

> "I called thee Father. I shewed thee more honour and respect than thou couldst have asked. Thee and thy sons I saved from a door-to-door life among the Baluchis. Thy family and thy *haram* I freed from Ibrahim's prison-house. Three crores I gave thee on Tatar Khan's lands. What ill sayest thou I have done thee, that thus thou shouldst hang a sword on thy either side, lead an army out, fall on lands of ours, and stir up strife and trouble?"

The reproach struck home: the old rebel was too ashamed to speak. Yet Babur contented himself with placing his enemy under the surveillance of a trusty adherent, Khwaja Mir-i-miran. Daulat Khan subsequently died a natural death at Sultanpur.

Babur's forceful personality and his capacity for surmounting difficulties were fully recognised by his own adherents. When the mob commenced rioting in the streets of Kabul in 1504, his Mirzas and Begs summoned him with the message, "Unless you come yourself, there will be no holding these people in." The emperor gallops at once to the scene, orders two or three rioters to be shot and two or three to be cut to pieces, and so stamps out the *émeute*. He never allowed his temper to be ruffled by such troubles; in every crisis he preserved his equanimity. His cousin Haidar records that during the grave rebellion in Kabul, which might well have provoked anger, passion or despair, the emperor remained "gay, generous, affectionate, simple and gentle." Mark his tranquillity also in the face of the desperate challenge thrown down by Rana Sanga and the Rajput clans, when his own men were deserting in terror and bad news was daily reaching him from all quarters. "We gave attention to none of them," he writes, "but went straight on with our own affair." And when his tactical genius and his imperturbable faith in Providence and his own right arm have given him the victory, he turns, as usual, to literary composition for the relief of his spirit and indites the following quatrain upon the final struggle of his military career:—

> For Islam's sake I wandered in the wilds,
> Prepared for war with Pagans and Hindus,
> Resolved myself to meet the martyr's death.
> Thanks be to God! a *ghazi* I became.

One more scene may form the fitting conclusion of this chapter. Babur, now King of Delhi, is spending the hot weather at Agra. The country is not yet pacified; the people are hostile; the roads round Agra are beset with thieves and robbers; grain and fodder are difficult to procure; many of Babur's men succumb to the excessive heat. The army is mutinous, remembering the cool climate and peace of Kabul, and makes preparations to leave India. Babur rises once more to the occasion:—

"When I knew of this unsteadiness amongst my people, I summoned all the Begs and took counsel. Said I, 'There is no supremacy and grip on the world without means and resources; without lands and retainers, sovereignty and command are impossible. By the labours of several years, by encountering hardships, by long travel, by flinging myself and the army into battle, and by deadly slaughter, we, through God's grace, beat these masses of enemies, in order that we might take their broad lands. And now what force compels us, what necessity has arisen that we should, without cause, abandon countries taken at such risk of life? Was it for us to remain in Kabul, the sport of harsh poverty? Henceforth, let no well-wisher of mine speak of such things! But let not those turn back from going, who, weak in strong persistence, have set their faces to depart!'"

This exhortation put his hearers to shame, and the army returned to its allegiance. But one man, Khwaja Kalan, so hated Hindustan that, much to Babur's annoyance, he elected to return to the north. Being, however, a tried soldier and a man of great influence and ability, he was appointed governor of Ghazni. At the moment of his departure he aggravated his offence in Babur's eyes by writing the following couplet on the wall of his residence at Delhi:—

> If safe and sound I cross the Sind,
> Blacken my face ere I wish for Hind.

Vexed at what he regarded as a breach of taste and good manners, Babur replied by sending him the following *extempore* verse:—

> Give a hundred thanks, Babur, that the generous Pardoner
> Hath given thee Sind and Hind and many a kingdom.
> If thou (i.e. Khwaja Kalan) hast not the strength for their heats,
> Remember the frost and ice that numbed thee of old in Ghazni.

Lane-Poole regards Babur's bold resolution to stay where he was, in the middle of India, among a hostile people and a discontented soldiery, as one of the most heroic acts of his career. Nor was his firmness baulked of its meet reward. The army gradually forgot its grievances; the tide of Indian opinion turned in favour of one, whose virtues and capabilities were self-evident. He who commanded their obedience was no longer the young prince of Farghana, fighting for his heritage, but a Man who had met with Triumph and Disaster and had learnt to "treat those two impostors just the same;" who had talked with crowds and kept his virtue; had walked with kings and not lost the common touch; a Man, indeed, who was master of himself and therefore, also, of the world around him. Hindustan accepted his authority; and so long as he was alive, she had no reason to regret her choice.

CHAPTER III

WINE, WOMAN AND SONG

"*O Believers! surely wine and games of chance and statues and the divining arrows, are an abomination of Satan's work! Avoid them, that ye may prosper.*

"*Only would Satan sow hatred and strife among you, by wine and games of chance, and turn you aside from the remembrance of God and from prayer; will ye not, therefore, abstain from them?*"—

The Koran.

DESPITE the Koranic injunction, wine-drinking to excess was almost universal throughout the East during the fifteenth century, and offered ample justification of Gibbon's remark that the wines of Shiraz have always prevailed over the law of the Prophet. By the time they reached India, the Musalmans had in great measure learnt to disregard the rules of Muhammad prohibiting the use of wine and other liquors.

Babur was no exception to the general body of Muslim princes, albeit he strictly eschewed wine and other intoxicants until about 1512, when he was nearly thirty years old. Thereafter, as his *Memoirs* tell us, he drank regularly and sometimes heavily until his forty-fourth year, taking the greatest pleasure in holding *symposia* with his intimate friends and comrades amid the orange-groves or beside the murmuring streams of Kabul. How strict an abstainer he was during his earlier years, can be ascertained from his narrative of the entertainment offered to him by the Mirzas at Herat in the year 1506-07:—

> "Two divans had been set in the north *shah-nishin*, facing each other, and with their sides turned to the north. On one Muzaffar Mirza and I sat, on the other Sultan Masud Mirza and Jahangir Mirza. We being guests, Muzaffar Mirza gave me place above himself. The social cups were filled, the cup-bearers ordered to carry them to the guests; the guests drank down the mere wine as if it were water-of-

life; when it mounted to their heads, the party waxed warm.

"They thought to make me also drink and to draw me into their own circle. Though up till then I had not committed the sin of wine-drinking and known the cheering sensation of comfortable drunkenness, I was inclined to drink wine and my heart was drawn to cross that stream. I had no inclination for wine in my childhood; I knew nothing of its cheer and pleasure. If, as sometimes, my father pressed wine on me, I excused myself; I did not commit the sin. After he died, Khwaja Kazi's right guidance kept me guiltless; as at that time I abstained from forbidden viands, what room was there for the sin of wine? Later on, when with the young man's lusts and at the prompting of sensual passion, desire for wine arose, there was no one to press it on me, no one indeed aware of my leaning towards it; so that, inclined for it though my heart was, it was difficult of myself to do such a thing, one thitherto undone.

> "It crossed my mind now, when the Mirzas were so pressing and when too we were in a town so refined as Heri, 'where should I drink if not here? here where all the chattels and utensils of luxury and comfort are gathered and in use.' So saying to myself, I resolved to drink wine; I determined to cross that stream; but it occurred to me that as I had not taken wine in Badiuz-zaman Mirza's house or from his hand, who was to me as an elder brother, things might find way into his mind, if I took wine in his younger brother's house and from his hand. Having so said to myself, I mentioned my doubt and difficulty. Said they, 'Both the excuse and the obstacle are reasonable,' pressed me no more to drink then, but settled that when I was in company with both Mirzas, I should drink under the insistence of both."

The earliest indication in the *Memoirs* that Babur had, in his own phrase, "crossed the stream" which divides observance of the commandments of Islam from transgression, belongs to the year 1519, when there was a wine-party in Khwaja Kalan's house. Thereafter the references to this indulgence become more numerous, and sometimes throw amusing side-lights on the behaviour of Babur's fellow-topers, who did not all possess as strong a head as his. Thus he writes:—

> "Near the Evening Prayer there was a wine-party, at which most of the household were present. After a time Kasim Beg's sister's son, Gadai 'the happy,' used very disturbing words, and being drunk, slid down on the cushion by my side. So Gadai Taghai picked him up and carried him out from the party."

On July 9th, 1519, there was a wine-party on the terrace-roof of the pigeon-house between the Afternoon and Evening Prayers. "Rather late a few horsemen were observed. . . . It was made out to be Darvesh-i-Muhammad Sarban on his way to me as the envoy of Mirza Khan. We shouted to him from the roof

'Drop the envoy's forms and ceremonies! Come! Come without formality!' He came and sat down in the company. He was then obedient and did not drink. Drinking went on till the end of the evening." The very terseness of Babur's prose brings this inimitable scene more clearly before us—the envoy, with his cavalry escort, approaching the capital of the ruler of Kabul after a weary ride across hill and valley; musing perhaps, as he rides forward, on matters of high politics. Suddenly a cry is heard; he looks up at the battlements and sees the potentate, to whom he is accredited, amid his boon companions, genially shouting to him to shed his ambassadorial dignity and join the drinking-circle. Though the envoy himself declines the proffered wine-cup, his presence serves as an excuse for a prolonged carouse by his host and the rest of the company.

Mrs. Beveridge justly remarks that many of Babur's lapses from the letter of the Koranic law were "from a Western standpoint very venial, and that his behaviour was no worse than that of the ordinarily temperate Westerner." Most of his drinking-bouts were brief interludes in a period of strenuous military achievement or prolonged physical strain, which could not have been undertaken or sustained by an habitual drunkard. The details which he gives of his entertainments clearly show that he drank like a gentleman, and was usually sober enough to remark all that took place, and pass judgment on those who exceeded the limits of decorum. Moreover, he scrupulously forbore to press wine upon a non-drinker, extending to others in his unregenerate days the same consideration which his uncles, the Mirzas, had shown towards him during the lavish entertainment in Herat.

Sometimes the episodes, in which liquor figured, resulted from an inclination for new experiences, or from curiosity—a characteristic which re-appeared in a marked degree in his grandson Akbar, whose enquiring mind sought satisfaction in the constant study of industrial and mechanical arts and processes. During his invasion of Bajaur, for example, Babur discovers that the local tribes manufacture a special kind of beer. He and his warriors find it too bitter for their taste; and accordingly,

> "Asas, Hasan, and Masti on the other raft were ordered to drink some. They did so, and became quite drunk. Hasan set up a disgusting disturbance; Asas, very drunk, did such unpleasant things that we were most uncomfortable. I thought of having them put off on the far side of the water, but some of the others begged them off."

An apt example of *experimentum in corpore vili*, which, we may be sure, was not repeated.

On another occasion Babur's curiosity led to a thoroughly Bohemian episode. On November 14th, 1519, he rode at midnight out of the Charbagh Palace at Kabul, dismissed the watchman and the groom who accompanied him, and about sunrise reached the underground conduit of Tardi Beg—"a choice spirit" according to Lane-Poole, "who began life as a dervish and ended as a distinguished general." Tardi Beg hurried forth to greet the emperor.

> "His love for a glass was well known to me: I had taken 100 *shahrukhis* (£5)

with me. These I gave him and bade him get wine and other things ready, as I had a fancy for a private and unrestrained party. He set out towards Bihzadi for wine, while I sent my horse by his slave to the valley-bottom and sat on the slope behind the conduit. At the first watch (9 a.m.) Tardi Beg brought a pitcher of wine, which we drank by turns. After him came Muhammad Kasim Barlas and Shahzada, who had learnt that he was fetching wine and had followed him, their minds quite empty of any idea of my presence. We invited them to the party. Said Tardi Beg. 'Hul-hul Aniga wishes to drink wine with you.' Said I, 'I have never seen a woman drink wine; call her in.' We also invited a qalandar (dervish) named Shahi, and one of the men belonging to the waterworks, who played the rebeck. There was drinking till the Evening Prayer on the rising ground behind the conduit; we then went into Tardi Beg's house and drank by lamp-light almost to the Bedtime Prayer. It was an amusing and guileless party. I

> lay down, while the others went to another house and drank there till beat of drum (midnight). Hul-hul Aniga came in and made me much disturbance. I got rid of her at last by flinging myself down as if drunk!"

Though the record gives no clue to the status and character of the lady, one may reasonably infer the nature of her profession. The spectacle of the emperor feigning to be dead drunk in order to escape the amorous attentions of the intoxicated woman, has a Rabelaisian flavour which must have determined Babur to forego further study of female intoxication.

The emperor did not apparently suffer in any way from this lapse at Tardi Beg's house, for he was up and astride his horse at the roll of the kettle-drum and had galloped to his first halt before sunrise. "He must have had an amazing constitution," writes Lane-Poole, "to survive this treatment." He was clearly able to carry a good deal of liquor without losing his senses or forgetting his manners; indeed he admits only twice in the course of his narrative that he was really the worse for drink. Describing an excursion during his first expedition from Kabul to Hindustan, he writes:—

> "We drank in the boat till the Bedtime Prayer; then getting off it, full of drink, we mounted, took torches in our hands, and went to camp from the river's bank, leaning over from our horses on this side, leaning over from that, at one loose-rein gallop! Very drunk I must have been, for when they told me next day that we had galloped loose-rein into camp, carrying torches, I could not recall it in the very least."

This escapade was followed on the return journey to Kabul by heavy drinking at Khwaja Hasan, where one of the party, Abdullah, in his intoxication threw himself into the river and was nearly frozen to death. He presented himself next day in a state of shivering repentance, and was given some forcible advice by Babur on his lack of self-control.

The emperor's indugence in the wine-cup

was often promoted by the beauty and splendour of Nature, and served as an outlet to the emotion stirred in him by the sight of "the falling petals of fruit-blossoms and the flame of autumn leaves." Lane-Poole remarks that "dissipation never dulled his appreciation of such delights or his pleasure in poetry and music;" and during his unregenerate days he kept his courage and his nerve, swimming every river that he met on his travels and hunting the rhinoceros and tiger in the midst of his wine-bibbing. Nor did his backslidings extinguish "that little spark of celestial fire called Conscience." Throughout his pursuit of pleasure and danger he cherished a sense of duty towards God and the Faith, which ultimately, in the greatest crisis of his life, brought about his final and complete abandonment of wine.

The renunciation took place in the dark and dubious hours preceding the struggle at Kanwaha with Rana Sanga, the leader of the Hindu confederacy and head of the chivalry of Mewar—the final conflict, indeed, which gave Babur the empire of Hindustan and the mastery of a realm extending from the Oxus to the frontier of Bengal and from the Himalaya to Gwalior. The story is best told in his own words:—

> "On Monday [February 25th, 1527] when I went out riding, I reflected as I rode that the wish to cease from sin had been always in my mind, and that my forbidden act had set a lasting stain upon my heart. Said I 'Oh! my soul!'

> How long wilt thou draw savour from sin?
> Repentance is not without savour, taste it!
> Through years how many has sin defiled thee?
> How much of peace has transgression given thee?
> How much hast thou been thy passion's slave?
> How much of thy life flung away?

> With the Ghazi's resolve since thou hast marched,
> Thou hast looked thine own death in the face!
> Who resolves to hold stubbornly fast to the death,
> Thou knowest what change he attains.

That far he removes him from all things
forbidden,
That from all his offences he cleanses himself,
With my own gain before me, I vowed to obey,
In this my transgression, the drinking of wine.

The flagons and cups of silver and gold, the
vessels of feasting,
I had them all brought;
I had them all broken up then and there,
Thus I eased my heart by renouncement of
wine.

"The fragments of the gold and silver vessels were distributed to deserving persons and to darweshes. The first to agree in renouncing wine was Asas; he had already agreed also about leaving his beard untrimmed. That night and next day some 300 Begs and persons of the household, soldiers and others, renounced wine. What wine we had with us was poured upon the ground; what Baba Dost had brought was ordered to be salted to make vinegar. At the place where the wine was poured upon the ground, a well was ordered to be dug, built up with stone and

> having an almshouse beside it. It was already finished in Muharram 935 (Sept. 1528), at the time I went to Sikri from Dholpur on my return from a visit to Gwalior."

Babur kept his vow and never again touched wine. That he found the fulfilment of his pledge no easy task, is plain from a sentence in a letter written a few years later to Khwaja Kalan. "The longing and craving for a wine-party" he wrote, "have been infinite and endless for two years past, so much so that sometimes the craving for wine brought me to the verge of tears. Thank God, this year that trouble has passed from my mind, perhaps by virtue of the blessing and entertainment of versifying the translation of the *Walidiyyah*." Babur never showed greater strength of mind and self-control than in thus keeping his vow in the face of constant temptation and the insidious promptings of his senses. The final conquest of self was facilitated by his whole-hearted devotion to literary pursuits.

Considering that the days of his youth and

manhood were spent in constant warfare and in expeditions and wanderings, which demanded the utmost physical endurance, it is hardly surprising that amorous dalliance played little part in Babur's life. After the manner of his race and age he married several wives—in all seven, and also kept two Circassian concubines, presented to him in 1526 by Shah Tahmasp of Persia. They subsequently became recognised ladies of the household and took part in domestic festivities and family conferences. By his seven legitimate spouses he had seventeen children, of whom eight died in childhood. Mahim Begam, who bore Humayun and four other children, and Gulrukh Begam, who also bore five children, were perhaps his favourite wives. For Ayesha, to whom he had been betrothed as a child in Samarkand, he confesses to having felt no passion, when he commenced to cohabit with her at Khujand in 1499.

> "Though I was not ill-disposed towards her, yet, this being my first marriage, out of modesty and bashfulness I used to see her once in 10, 18, or 20 days. Later on,

> when even my first inclination did not last, my bashfulness increased. Then my mother Khanim used to send me, once a month or every forty days, with driving and driving, dunnings and worryings."

A husband who has to be driven to his marital duties by the upbraiding of a female relative would not suit most women, and one is not surprised to learn from the *Memoirs* that Ayesha, who probably resented this frigid treatment, deserted Babur before the year 1503.

Babur cherished deep respect for his nomad-born grandmother, Aisan-daulat, for his mother Qutlug-nigar, who was a scholar's daughter, and for his sister Khanzada, who "proved her devotion to him during his years of trial." Of his grandmother he remarks that few can have rivalled her in judgment; "she was very wise and far-sighted, and most affairs of mine were carried through under her advice." He was always ready to sacrifice himself for the welfare of these women of his family: and when they were besieged in Andijan by Auzun Hassan and Sultan Ahmad Tambul in 1497-98 and sent him a plaintive prayer for deliverance, he rode at once from Samarkand to succour them, despite the fact that he had been seriously ill—so ill that for several days he could not speak—and that policy demanded his continued presence in Samarkand. In the hour of his poverty and abasement in Tashkend, he would not set forth, as he at first proposed, to try his fortune in China, until he knew that his mother was safely under the protection of her younger brother; and when he and his small band of comrades left Farghana for ever, as homeless exiles, he gave up for his mother's comfort and convenience the only tent he possessed.

This filial devotion must not blind us, however, to the fact that the emperor felt profound contempt for those who permitted women to interfere in politics or associated themselves with feminine intrigue. Nor did he suffer gladly a loquacious or quarrelsome woman. "She took herself for a sensible woman," he writes of Khadija Begam, mistress of Abu Said Mirza and, later, wife of Husain Baiqara, "but was a silly chatterer; may also have been a heretic"; and of another,

> "She was very cross-tempered and made the Mirza endure much wretchedness, until driven at last to despair, he set himself free by divorcing her. What was he to do? Right was with him—
>
> A bad wife in a good man's house
> Makes this world already his Hell.
>
> God preserve every Musalman from this misfortune! Would that not a single cross or ill-tempered wife were left in the world!"

To which pious hope every student of Babur's *Memoirs* will assuredly reply *Amen*. Babur pours scorn upon Zuhra Begi Agha, an Uzbeg woman, who promised Shaibani Khan that if he would take her to wife, her son should transfer to him the kingdom of Samarkand. Her immodest offer was accepted and brought about her degradation.

> "As for that calamitous woman, who in her folly gave her son's house and possessions to the winds in order to get herself a husband, Shaibani Khan cared not one atom for her, indeed did not regard her as the equal of a mistress or a concubine."

And as for her son, the Mirza, "having entered into a woman's affairs, he withdrew himself from the circle of men of good repute. . . . Of acts so shameful, no more should be heard." Shortly after giving up his territory, he was assassinated by Shaibani's orders.

While he was deeply attached to the brave, simple and devoted Mongol women of his family and deferential to women in general, Babur seems to have been "curiously insusceptible to the tender passion." Only in the case of Masuma, Ayesha's younger sister, does he appear to have reciprocated the love which she felt for him at first sight. "One day when I was visiting my Aka, Masuma Sultan Begam came there with her mother and at once felt arise in her a great inclination towards me." The betrothal, which was then and there arranged, was followed by her marriage to Babur at Kabul in 1507.

Likewise, except on one occasion in his youth, when his modesty provided a complete safeguard againt a fugitive attraction, Babur never felt the slightest inclination to pederasty and homo-sexual vice, which was tolerably prevalent in the Muhammadan society of his day. On the contrary he stigmatises it in plain language as abominable, and speaks with disgust of those who practised it. Consider, for example, his pen-portrait of Sultan Mahmud Mirza, great-grandson of Timur:—

> " He carried violence and vice to frantic excess, was a constant wine-bibber, and kept many catamites. If anywhere in his territory there was a handsome boy, he used by some means or other to have him brought for a catamite; of his Begs' sons and his sons' Begs' sons he made catamites, and laid command for this service on his very foster-brothers and on their own

> brothers. So common in his day was that vile practice, that no person was without his catamite; to keep one was thought a merit, not to keep one a defect. Through his infamous violence and vice, his sons died in the day of their strength."

He likewise attributes the early deaths of Sultan Husain Mirza's sons, numbering fourteen, of whom three only were born in legal wedlock, to the practice of vice and debauchery "by him, his sons, his tribes and hordes." In eulogising a warrior named Sayyidim for his admirable military and social qualities, Babur adds, "his fault was that he practised vice and pederasty": he stigmatises his first guardian, Shaikh Majid Beg, "excellent in rule and method," as a vicious person who kept catamites: one of the principal courtiers of Sultan Husain Mirza of Herat is labelled "impudent and prodigal, a keeper of catamites, a constant dicer and draught player." It is probable, also, that one cause of Babur's intense dislike of the treacherous Khusrau Shah, Amir of Sultan

Mahmud Mirza, was the fact that Khusrau had been a catamite in his youth.

There is no word about prostitution in Babur's autobiography; and in view of the engaging candour with which he records his own thoughts and acts, one may infer that he never sought the embraces of a harlot. That others were in this respect less scrupulous, may be gathered from Babur's description of Khwaja Abdullah Marwarid, who was at one time Chief Justice of Herat and afterwards one of Mirza Husain's principal courtiers. A highly accomplished man, he was an expert performer on the dulcimer, a fine calligraphist, and a charming poet. But "vicious and shameless, he became the captive of a sinful disease through his vicious excesses, outlived his hands and feet, tasted the agonies of torture for several years, and departed from the world under that affliction." We have here an early and illuminating reference to the effects of syphilis, which apparently was as prevalent then as it is to-day in the bazaars of the Orient. Babur lived far too vigorous and hard a life to run any such risk, and even in his days of intemperance never drank enough to lose control of his passions, as the drunken Hul-hul Aniga discovered after the party at Tardi Beg's quarters.

Like all the Timurids, Babur was fond of music and was himself a composer of songs, to one of which—in four time—he refers in his diary for January, 1520. He frequently mentions the names of skilful performers on the flute, dulcimer, guitar, lute and harp; he could appreciate the *technique* of airs composed by a fine musician like Banai of Herat, who on one occasion in Samarkand wrote a song on Babur's name. Vocal and instrumental performances were a recognised feature of the emperor's wine-parties. "His friends," writes Lane-Poole, "would gather round him under the *Tal* trees, among the orange-groves or beside a canal; the musicians played and they drank till they were merry. It was a rule that every man who sang a Persian song—one of Babur's own composition, sometimes—should have his glass, and everyone who sang a Turki song, another: but on rare occasions it was enacted that if a man became drunk, he must be removed, and another take his place." Babur's musical taste was as cultivated as his taste for letters, and bad singing he could not tolerate. In his account of the entertainment provided by the Mirzas at Herat he remarks:—

> "At the party among the musicians was Hafiz Haji; Jalal-ud-din Muhammad, the flautist, was there too, and the younger brother of Ghulam Shadi, who played the harp. Hafiz Haji sang well, as Herat people sing, quietly, delicately, and in tune. With Jahangir Mirza was a Samarkandi singer, Mir Jan, whose singing was always loud, harsh, and out of tune. The Mirza, who was far gone in his cups, ordered him to sing, and sing he did, loudly, harshly, and without taste. The men of Khurasan pride themselves on their good breeding; but many stopped their ears, some frowned; yet out of respect for the Mirza none ventured to stop him."

It was doubtless from Babur that Akbar, Jahangir and Shah Jahan inherited their taste for vocal and instrumental performances.

Akbar, as Abul Fazl informs us, took lessons in singing from a Hindu *maestro* and harmonised a large number of Persian airs. He also secured the services of Tansen, originally a Hindu of Gwalior, who was reputed to be the finest singer ever heard in India. Jahangir maintained a very large body of male and female singers, who were grouped in parties, one for every day of the week. Shah Jahan, as the chronicles of his reign relate, possessed a fine and well-trained voice and often sang himself at the musical *soirées* in the Diwan-i-Khas at Delhi. The encouragement given to all forms of music by the emperors in the heyday of the Mughal empire must be regarded as a legacy of the taste for melody which brightened Babur's scanty leisure hours and enhanced the lure of the wine-cup.

> Here with a little bread beneath the bough,
> A flask of wine, a book of verse, and thou
> Beside me, singing in the wilderness,
> Ah! wilderness were Paradise enow.

Thus did wine and song rythmically fill the pauses of the stern years of war and hardship.

Though merely interludes in the tale of perilous adventure, these *symposia* helped to buoy the spirits of the emperor and his circle, and perchance also to inspire those feelings of clemency, which, in contrast with the military practice of the time, Babur often displayed towards delinquents and captives. Wine and song in truth were at once the natural complement and the token of his inexhaustible geniality.

CHAPTER IV

ART AND NATURE

"*Non omnis moriar, multaque pars mei*
Vitabit Libitinam."

LANE-POOLE has stated that "Babur's place in history rests upon his Indian conquests, which opened the way for an imperial line; but his place in biography and in literature is determined rather by his daring adventures and persevering efforts in his earlier days, and by the delightful *Memoirs* in which he related them. Soldier of fortune as he was, Babur was not the less a man of fine literary taste and fastidious critical perception. In Persian, the language of culture, the Latin of Central Asia, as it is of India, he was an accomplished poet, and in his native Turki he was master of a pure and unaffected style alike in prose and verse." His faculty for literary composition was, no doubt, partly inherited: for Timur himself wrote annals in Turki; Timur's grandson, Ulugh Beg, was the author of two works; Ulugh Khan's two sons were distinguished, the one as a poet, the other as a prose-writer. Moreover, he had before him the example of Sultan Husain Baiqara, the Timurid ruler of Herat, a great patron of art and letters, whose court was thronged by the intellectual spirits of the age. Yet it is questionable whether any previous member of the Timurid family possessed literary talents equal to Babur's, or acquired an equal mastery of Turki prose. Great natural intelligence, an enquiring mind, a sense of humour, and good taste combined to render Babur's work unique; and when we remember that his literary activity was cultivated amid an unending series of military and political vicissitudes, we are fain to subscribe whole-heartedly to his cousin Mirza Haidar's eulogy of Babur's "many virtues and numberless excellences."

Considering his strenuous and adventurous life the volume of his written works is no less remarkable than their quality. They include, according to the list prepared by Mrs. Beveridge, the miscellaneous verse quoted in the *Babur-nama;* a *divan* or collection of poems sent to

Pulad Sultan in 1519; a diary for 1519-20; the *Mubin*, a treatise on Moslem Law in 2,000 lines of Turki verse, composed in 1522 for the benefit of his son Kamran; a treatise on prosody written in 1524; poems written in Hindustan; the *Babur-nama*, his autobiographical *Memoirs;* and the *Walidiyyah-risala*, a metrical translation of Khwaja Obaidullah Ahrari's *Parental Tract*, composed in 1528-29. The genesis of the last-named work is ascribed by Babur in his *Memoirs* to an attack of fever which laid him low in November, 1528.

> "I trembled less on Sunday. During the night of Tuesday it occurred to me to versify the *Walidiyyah-risala* of His Reverence Khwaja Obaidullah. I laid it to heart that if I, going to the soul of His Reverence for protection, was freed from this disease, it would be a sign that my poem was accepted, just as the author of the *Qasidatu'l-burda* was freed from the affliction of paralysis, when his poem had been accepted. To this end I began to versify the tract, using the metre of

> Maulana Abdur Rahim Jami's *Subhatu'l-ahrar* (Rosary of the Righteous). Thirteen couplets were made in the same night. I tasked myself to make not fewer than ten a day; in the end one day had been omitted."

The *Babur-nama* or autobiography, which has been described as "fit to rank with the confessions of St. Augustine and Rousseau and the memoirs of Gibbon and Newton," is unfortunately not wholly complete, the annals and diary of the years 1508 to 1519 having disappeared. The loss of the relevant sheets may, as Mrs. Beveridge suggests, have occurred during the vicissitudes of Humayun's fourteen years of exile from the throne of Delhi; and some pages may perhaps have been destroyed during the monsoon storm of 1529, which Babur describes as follows:—

> "That same night . . . such a storm burst, in the inside of a moment, from the up-piled clouds of the Rainy Season, and such a stiff gale arose that few tents were

> left standing. I was in the Audience-tent, about to write: before I could collect papers and sections, the tent came down with its porch, right on my head. The *tungluq* (flap in tent-roof) went to pieces. God preserved me! No harm befell me! Sections and book were drenched under water and gathered together with much difficulty. We laid them in the folds of a woollen throne-carpet, put this on the throne, and on it piled blankets. . . . We, without sleep, were busy till shoot of day drying folios and sections."

The salient feature of the *Babur-nama* is its honesty. The conviction grows, as we read it, that it contains the truth, the whole truth, and nothing but the truth. In describing the favours he had bestowed upon his Chaghatai relatives and the sorry manner in which they were requited, he remarks:—

> "I do not write this in order to make complaint; I have written the plain truth. I do not set down these matters in order to

> make known my own deserts; I have set down exactly what happened. In this history I have held firmly to it that the truth should be reached in every matter, and that every act should be recorded precisely as it occurred. From this it follows that I have set down of good and bad whatever is known concerning father and elder brother, kinsman and stranger; of them all I have set down carefully the known virtues and defects."

Again, when he pens a few words of pardonable pride on his capture of Samarkand at the age of nineteen, he repudiates any idea of magnifying his own achievement. In his own phrase "the truth is set down;" and our acceptance of that statement is amply justified by the fact that in the course of the work he never excuses his own mistakes and failures, nor slurs in the smallest degree over his own lapses from grace.

Babur's prose style was suited to his blunt and open nature. The flowery phraseology and hyperbole, so common in Eastern literature, find no place in his autobiography, which is written in clear, simple, terse language, void of superfluous words. His descriptions of the countries in which his lot was cast—their climate, fauna, flora, products, water-supply, population, trade and so forth, are models of what such compositions should be—never prolix, but containing all the details that a stranger, traveller, or student might wish to know. The following extract from a letter which he wrote to Humayun proves that he aimed at simplicity of expression and disliked slipshod composition:—

> "Thou hast written me a letter, as I ordered thee to do. But why not have read it over? If thou hadst thought of reading it, thou couldst not have done it, and, unable thyself to read it, wouldst certainly have made alterations in it. Though by taking trouble it can be read, it is very puzzling, and who ever saw an enigma in prose? Thy spelling, though not bad, is not quite correct. . . . Although thy letter can be

> read if every sort of pains be taken, yet it cannot be quite understood because of that obscure wording of thine. Thy remissness in letter writing seems to be due to the thing which makes thee obscure, that is to say, to elaboration. In future, write without elaboration; use plain clear words. So will thy trouble and thy reader's be less."

Could a modern educationist have given better advice than this on epistolary style? Incidentally the letter reminds us that Babur was no mean calligraphist. The art of fine writing has always been highly esteemed in India, Persia, and China; and the penmanship of a manuscript was often considered more valuable and more important than its illustrations. The dictum of Horace—*Poeta nascitur non fit*—aptly expresses the view prevalent in Asiatic lands of the genius of the *Khushnavis* or fine writer, whose handiwork was collected and preserved in albums as carefully as the finest specimens of pictorial art. Broadly speaking, the various modes of writing were distinguished from one another by differences in the proportions of the straight and curved lines, and one mode at least was a combination of two of the older styles. Babur invented a new handwriting, which he calls *Baburi Khatt*, and wrote a copy of the Koran in it, which he afterwards sent to Mecca. He mentions that he showed the script and explained its special features to one of the Kazis at Herat, who then and there wrote some sentences in it.

The *Babur-nama* reveals its author's talent for delineating character in a few words. The portrait of Sultan Husain Mirza of Herat, for example, is admirable: two short paragraphs lay bare his personal appearance, his virtues and his failings. Equally illuminating are the accounts of Sultan Ahmad Mirza and the Amirs of Umar Shaikh's court. One of the latter was "a good-natured and simple person, who used to improvise very well at drinking-parties;" another was "worthless by nature and habit, a stingy, severe, strife-stirring person, false, self-pleasing, rough of tongue and cold of face;" of a third he writes, "in management and equipment excellent, and took good care of his men. He prayed not, he kept no fasts, he was like a heathen, and he was a tyrant." There were also Mir Ghyas, "a laugher, a joker, and fearless in vice," and Qambar Ali the Mughal—"Till he was a made man, his conduct was excellent. Once he arrived, he was slack. He was full of talk and of foolish talk—a great talker is sure to be a foolish one—his capacity was limited and his brain muddy." A brief sketch of Jani Beg, one of Ahmad Mirza's nobles, throws a sidelight upon the rude manners of the times:—

> "While he (Jani Beg) was governor in Samarkand, an envoy came to him from the Uzbegs, renowned for his strength. An Uzbeg is said to call a strong man a bull *(bukuh)*. 'Are you a *bukuh?*' said Jani Beg to the envoy; 'if you are, come, let's have a friendly wrestle together.' Whatever objections the envoy raised, he refused to accept. They wrestled, and Jani Beg gave the fall. He was a brave man."

There is many a happy touch in his picture

of Husain Baiqara's court. One noble was mad on chess; "he played it according to his own fancy, and, if others play with one hand, he played with both. Avarice and stinginess ruled in his character." Another wrote verse of all sorts, filled "with terrifying words and mental images;" when he recited one of his couplets to Jami, the latter "asked him whether he was reciting verse or frightening people." Then there was the athletic spirit, who could take a flying leap over seven horses side by side, and "the curiously humble, disconsolate and harmless person, who seems to have had no equal in making riddles and to have given his whole time to it." Yet another, who was a Chief Justice, wrote a book which in the preface he declared to be Sultan Husain's "own written word and literary composition," while in the body of the book he wrote "all by the sub-signed author" above odes and verses well known to be his own. "A singularly absurd procedure," comments Babur, who clearly did not approve of "literary ghosts." He tells us also of Ali Sher, who besides being the best Turki poet of his day, was a fine soldier and leader of fashion. "Whenever anyone produced a novelty, he called it Ali Sher's, in order to give it credit and vogue. Some things were called after him in compliment, e.g., when he had ear-ache and wrapped his head in one of the blue triangular kerchiefs women tie over their heads in winter, that kerchief was called Ali Sher's comforter." Banai the poet, critic, and calligraphist, whose jokes sometimes got him into trouble, raised a laugh by inventing a new pad for his ass and calling it "the Ali Sher donkey-pad."

Babur's sense of humour must have been equally tickled by the tale which he recounts of the Sultan of Bajaur and his mother's corpse:—

> "All through the hill country above Multa-Kundi . . . it is said that when a woman dies and has been laid on a bier, she, if she has not been an ill-doer, gives the bearers such a shake, when they lift the bier by its four sides, that against their will and hindrance her corpse falls to the ground; but if she has done ill, no movement occurs. This was heard not only from

> Kunaris, but again and again in Bajaur, Sawad, and the whole hill-tract. Haidar Ali Bajauri—a Sultan who governed Bajaur well—when his mother died, did not weep or betake himself to lamentation, or put on black, but said 'Go! lay her on the bier! if she move not, I will have her burned!' (i.e. treated like an infidel). They laid her on the bier; the desired movement followed; when he heard this was so, he put on black and betook himself to lamentation."

Many and diverse were the occasions which prompted Babur to commit his thoughts to verse. He would write an ode during a halt in camp; in the brief respite after his capture of Samarkand, he amused himself by writing Turki poems; he composed verses just before battle, or when enjoying a peaceful excursion by river with his comrades, or when lying ill with fever. The conjunction of New Year's Day with the *Id-ul-fitr*, during a return march to Kabul, formed the subject of a neat quatrain; while his failures and disasters often served as the occasion for a well-turned couplet. After the battle of Panipat, when Nizam Khan of Biana seemed indisposed to surrender, Babur sent him "royal letters of promise and threat," and drove his meaning home with an *extempore* Persian quatrain:—

> Strive not with the Turk, o Mir of Biana!
> His skill and his courage are obvious.
> If thou come not soon, nor give ear to counsel,—
> What need to detail what is obvious?

Babur's poetry, like his prose, was usually marked by good taste. He admits to having composed frivolous and jesting verse in his younger days, but the composition of the *Mubin* cured him of this weakness. "A pity it will be," he declares, "if the tongue which has treasure of utterances so lofty as these are, waste itself again on low words; sad will it be, if again vile imaginings find way into the mind, which has made exposition of these sublime realities." After that declaration he was guilty of only one lapse, when he wrote a somewhat improper couplet on Mulla Ali Jan: but, believing that an illness which attacked him a few days later was sent as a punishment for his backsliding, he broke his pen in token of repentance and thenceforth faithfully avoided anything approaching ribaldry. Thus he was neither hypocritical nor insincere, when he openly condemned the poet Hilali for composing an ode on the immoral love of a darwesh for a king. Babur was greatly incensed at the thought that anyone "for the sake of a few elegant quatrains should describe a young man, and that young man a king, as resembling the shameless and immoral."

During his restless years of adventure Babur managed to indulge his artistic tastes in other directions. Although few of his buildings now survive, he set an example of architectural activity, which ultimately fructified in the magnificent buildings of his Mughal descendants. As early as 1496, when he was thirteen years old, he built a porched retreat in Ush; in 1505 he embellished a saint's tomb at Ghazni with a dome, and excavated a domed chamber in the rock at Kandahar; he constructed a mosque, caravanserai, and hot baths in Kabul. But it was after his arrival in India that he really applied himself to building, and summoned from Constantinople pupils of the famous Albanian architect Sinan, who had designed many important buildings in the Ottoman empire. He states in the *Memoirs* that 680 Indian masons worked daily on his buildings at Agra, and that nearly 1,500 were daily employed on his buildings at Sikri, Biana, Gwalior and other places. Two only of his buildings now survive—a mosque built at Panipat in 1526 to commemorate his victory, and another mosque erected on the site of an ancient temple of Rama in Oudh, which he destroyed in 1528 as a symbol of paganism. The latter mosque bears an inscription, which runs thus:—

> By order of the Emperor Babur, whose justice is an edifice reaching to the very height of heaven,
>
> The good-hearted Mir Baqi built this alighting place of angels.
>
> May this goodness last for ever! The year of building was likewise made clear when I said—*Buvad Khair baqi* (= A.H. 935)!

PLANE TREE AVENUE IN BABUR'S BURIAL GARDEN

From Atkinson's Sketches in Afghanistan by permission of the India Office

Babur's greatest contribution to India's adornment was his introduction of the art of garden planning and construction, which had reached the people of Central Asia through Persia in very early days and had been fully developed in Turkestan. Babur was passionately devoted to gardens or "paradises," as they might more aptly be styled, with their climbing terraces, fountains, and dwarf-waterfalls, flanked by parterres of shrubs and many-hued flowers. He built at least ten gardens in Kabul, including the one which contains his grave, and the "Garden of Fidelity," in which, as he tells us, oranges, citrons and pomegranates grew in abundance. "Those were the days of the garden's beauty," he writes after a visit to the latter; "its lawns were one sheet of clover; its pomegranate trees yellowed to autumn splendour, their fruit full red; fruit on the orange-trees green and glad, countless oranges, but not yet as yellow as our hearts desired." Another favourite spot was the "Fountain of the Three Friends," round which he made an irrigated pleasaunce. "If the world over," he exclaims, "there is a place to match this when the *arghwans* (Judas-trees) are in full bloom, I do not know it." After fixing on Agra as his capital in India, he commenced to lay out the Ram Bagh on the banks of the Jumna, which afterwards became a favourite retreat of the Empress Nur Jahan. In it he built reservoirs, baths and pavilions, and sowed the beds with roses and narcissus. His horticultural taste and knowledge must have been considerable: areca nut palms, which he planted in one of the Agra gardens, had reached a height of 90 feet in the reign of his great-grandson; in another which he named the "Flower-scatterer," he obtained hundreds of pine apples yearly and feasted his eyes on a wealth of crimson oleanders, which he had transplanted from Gwalior; he speaks in another place of getting good grapes from the vines which he planted in the "Garden of Eight Paradises."

"How fair," wrote Disraeli in *Sybil*, "is a garden amid the toils and passions of existence." A similar sentiment inspires many of Babur's references to the flowering paradises of Farghana and Kabul. No one worshipped natural beauty more ardently, or showed a keener appreciation of the loveliness of foliage and flowers. The mere sight of violets and roses in bloom arouses his emotion; he speaks with delight of a field of tulips of thirty-four different kinds, which he discovers one day among the Kabul foot-hills. India seems to him "charmless and disorderly," until he has planted gardens which may remind him of the witchery of that "Eden of verdure and blossom," Kabul in the spring-time; and as he thinks of the matchless charm of those northern retreats, he breaks into verse,

> My heart like the bud of the red, red rose,
>   Lies fold within fold aflame;
> Would the breath of even a myriad Springs
>   Blow my heart's bud to a rose?

Though he could not draw or paint, Babur possessed the true artist's vision for form and colour, as displayed in Nature's handiwork; and it was that vision, bequeathed to his descendants and transformed by the influence of their Indian environment, which found ultimate expression in the beautiful pictorial art of Jahangir's court and in the incomparable architectural master-pieces of Shah Jahan's reign. Akbar, a born king of men and one of the greatest sovereigns known to history, directly inherited his grandfather's love of gardens and flowers, and laid out many a flowering "abode of delight" at Fathpur-Sikri and elsewhere. How great a boon these Mughal gardens were to India, is now frankly recognised; and it is well to remember that the credit of first making the desert to blossom as the rose belongs to the simple-hearted, genial and courageous giant, who after many years of tribulation marched down through the north-western passes and laid in India the foundation of a magnificent imperial heritage.

CHAPTER V

THE LAST PHASE

"*Quique sui memores aliquos fecere merendo.*"

In June 1529, Babur's wife, Mahim Begam, mother of Humayun, arrived in Agra after a five months' journey from Kabul. She was followed shortly afterwards by his sister, Khanzada Begam, and his other wives, who had been despatched to India, in pursuance of Babur's express wish, by Khwaja Kalan, the emperor's friend and viceroy of Kabul and Ghazni. Thus re-united with his nearest relatives, Babur sought occasional relief from the heavy task of settling his new territories by paying visits with his family to Dholpur, Sikri, and other places within reach of Agra. It was on one of these excursions in 1529 that he showed signs of weariness for the first time, and expressed a wish to relinquish active control of public affairs. His daughter, Gulbadan Begam ("Princess Rosebody"), tells us that one day, when sitting with his family in the garden named "The Gold-scatterer," Babur declared that he was "bowed down with ruling and reigning" and longed to transfer his sovereignty to Humayun, in order that he might retire to that garden with a single attendant and end his days in peace. One is fain to believe that the wish was only transitory, born of the contrast between the physical and mental strain of more than thirty years' fighting and leadership and the tranquillity of the fair garden, which owed its very existence to his deep love of natural beauty. Babur was surely too sincere to resile from the advice which he himself had given to Humayun in a letter of November 27th, 1528:—

> "Neglect not the work chance has brought; slothful life in retirement befits not sovereign rule."

He was not the man to shirk responsibility or, like a Hindu *sanyasi*, withdraw himself prematurely from active intercourse with the world.

But, had he known it, the hour of his release was drawing near, to be preceded by an act of self-surrender, which signally exemplifies his affection for his own flesh and blood and his abiding faith in the power and mercy of God. Towards the close of the year 1530, as related in the later chronicles of Gulbadan Begam and Abul Fazl, Humayun, in his fief of Sambhal, was stricken by a malignant type of fever, which defied all efforts to subdue it. In the hope, perhaps, of more speedy cure, he was brought by river to Agra, his mother meeting him *en route* at Mathura. But the change of scene brought no improvement; the highest medical skill available at Agra gave no relief. Then Babur, in desperate anxiety for the safety of his chosen heir, bethought him of a rite, which has always been deemed in the East a sovereign means of saving a valued life, and which consists of solemn intercession and the offer by the suppliant of his most precious possession in exchange for the life of the sufferer. The emperor's courtiers and others suggested the presentation of the famous diamond, the *Koh-i-Nur*, as a meet pledge for Humayun's recovery: but Babur, who valued his son's life more highly than all the jewels and fine gold of Al-Hind, determined to place his own life in the balance. In the name of a Muslim saint he prayed long and fervently for the consummation of his wish, and then moved thrice round Humayun's sick-bed, saying aloud, "O God! if a life may be exchanged for a life, I, who am Babur, give my life and my being for Humayun." Even as he spoke, he felt the fever grip him and knew that his prayer had been answered. In an ecstacy of grateful joy he cried a second time, "I have borne it away, I have borne it away;" and he went out from the presence of Humayun straight to his own couch, from which he never rose again. Humayun was saved and returned convalescent to Sambhal: Babur, forfeiting his life by this final act of self-sacrifice, died a few weeks afterwards.

The modern sceptic may decline to believe the story as told by Babur's daughter and by his grandson's courtly biographer, and may ascribe to mere coincidence the recovery of Humayun and the simultaneous illness of his father, whose health had certainly suffered from years of strain and exposure. But to the mind of the believer in divine intervention this view takes inadequate account of Babur's invincible will and of his genuine faith in a Higher Power. Like one of the greatest of Carlyle's *Heroes*, "he believed wholly in his Faith, fronting Time with it and Eternity with it": and peradventure the fulfilment of the prayer, offered with inflexible purpose and unswerving trust, was the recompense vouchsafed by Allah the Merciful and Compassionate to the sincerity and self-abnegation of his royal suppliant.

So the scene changes to the emperor's chamber. As soon as it was evident that Babur was sinking, Humayun, now restored to full vigour, was hastily summoned from Sambhal and arrived in Agra four days before the end. On the day of his arrival, the dying Padshah summoned his chiefs and counsellors before him for the last time, and charged them to acknowledge Humayun as his successor—"Fail not in loyalty towards him," said he; "I hope in God that he on his part will bear himself well towards men." Then addressing Humayun, he bade him practise liberality and justice, seek the favour of God, cherish and protect his subjects, accept apologies from those who had failed in duty, and grant pardon to transgressors. "Moreover," he added, "I commit you and your brethren and all my kinsfolk and your people and my people to God's keeping and entrust them all to you. And the cream of my last behest is this, 'Do naught against your brothers, even though they may deserve it.'"

Can it be that in his last hours Babur foresaw the ruin which fratricidal hatred and jealousy were destined to bring upon his dynasty? Was there vouchsafed to him some dim prophetic vision of the blinding of Shahryar, the murders of Khusru and of the young sons of Daniyal, the tragic fate of Dara Shikoh? Surely not so. But he knew enough of Kamran's nature to realise that the latter, though hitherto well-behaved, was quite capable of disloyalty to Humayun, and by virtue of his experience he must have been aware that fraternal discord was a natural result of the polygamous system followed by the rulers of his age and country. It is certain, at any rate, that the atrophy of all natural affection, which fell like a blight upon the imperial family after the death of Akbar, was disastrous to Mughal sovereignty, and that had Babur's successors in the seventeenth and eighteenth centuries emulated his standard of domestic affection and staunch loyalty to kinsfolk, they would have obviated one of the main causes of the rapid decline of their political supremacy.

The final call came on Monday, December 26th, 1530; and with the words "Lord, I am here for Thee," Babur passed quietly away amid the lamentations of his children and relatives. Khwaja Kalan, his friend of many years, expressed the public grief in the following lines of his elegy:—

> Alas! that time and the changeful heaven should exist without thee;
> Alas! and Alas! that time should remain and thou shouldst be gone.

Babur had left written instructions for his burial in Kabul; but for the time being his body was entombed in the Aram Bagh ("Garden of Rest"), opposite the present site of the Taj

Mahal. A guardian of the grave was appointed; reciters were chosen to lead the daily prayers enjoined by Islam and to intercede for the soul of the dead ruler; and the revenues of Sikri, together with a contribution from Biana, were allocated for the maintenance of the tomb. Some time, however, between 1539 and 1544 his remains were conveyed to Kabul and there buried in a fair garden, on the slope of the Shah-i-Kabul hill, which he had chosen himself as his last resting-place. According to his wish, the grave lies open to the sky—a simple unadorned covering that needs no doorkeeper. The walled garden, which forms its setting, with its fifteen terraces and its twelve dwarf waterfalls, looks forth over the plain to the dark hills and the eternal snows, and by means of a walled enclosure adjacent to its ornamental gateway provides the poor and destitute with shelter from the weather. Babur's earnest desire for communion with Nature, even after death, was inherited by his great-grandson, Jahangir, who wished to be buried in his favourite garden in Kashmir, and asked almost with his last breath that his grave might lie open to the heavens and

BABUR'S GRAVE

From Atkinson's Sketches in Afghanistan, by permission of the India Office

be watered by the rain and the dew. Both these Timurids, though their characters and fortunes were so different, were possessed of a passionate admiration for "the green mosaic pavements and strange carpentry and arras-work of this noble palace of a world."

The tomb soon became a place of pilgrimage for Babur's descendants, who did much to improve and beautify the surroundings. The small marble mosque, which crowned one of the terraces, was the tribute of Shah Jahan; but perhaps the fairest offering to the memory of the illustrious dead was the inscription, composed by Jahangir, which is graven upon the white marble slab at the head of the grave. Thus run the verses of the legend:—

> A Ruler from whose brow shone the Light of God, was that Backbone of the Faith, Muhammad Babur Padshah. Together with majesty, dominion, fortune, rectitude, the open hand and the firm Faith, he had share in prosperity, abundance, and the triumph of victorious arms. He won the material world and became a moving

> light; for his every conquest he looked, as for Light, towards the world of Souls. When Paradise became his dwelling, and Ruzwan [doorkeeper of Paradise] asked me the date, I gave him for answer "Paradise is for ever Babur Padshah's abode."

Here then we bid adieu to Babur, the founder of the Mughal dynasty of India. He was not quite forty-eight years old at the hour of his death; but during that brief span of life he had scaled the heights of success and plumbed the very depths of misfortune. He graduated in the school of adversity, for his boyhood was spent in one continuous effort to save his ancestral kingdom from the covetous onslaughts of Mongol and Uzbeg clansmen: and when, after twenty years' indomitable struggle, he realised that Heaven had decreed his failure, he turned his eyes, ever alight with deathless hope, towards a new world and a greater empire.

> "*Tu ne cede malis, sed contra audentior ito,*
> *Quam tua te Fortuna sinet.*"

That was the spirit which inspired Babur in his exile—which carried him victorious from the snows of Turkestan to the sunlit banks of the Jumna.

That Babur was ambitious, none will deny; indeed he himself admits it. Yet what man of superlative courage and vigour is not so? That his punishments were sometimes cruel, that he had little or no regard for the sanctity of human life, is equally true. Yet allowance must be made for the spirit and manners of his age and for the influence of heredity. Babur never slew men wantonly, as did some of his Muslim contemporaries and predecessors, albeit in his veins flowed the blood both of Chenghiz Khan, the scourge of Asia, and of the murderer of seventeen million men, who sleeps beneath the blue dome of Samarkand. He never exhibited the savage caprice of an Asiatic despot, and more than once in the course of his *Memoirs* he expresses his hatred of vice, tyranny and cruelty.

Whatever Babur's failings may have been, they were far outweighed by his good qualities. In the phrase of Carlyle, he was "a born indefeasible gentleman." A good sportsman, fond of all field sports and warlike amusements, his physical vigour and endurance were remarkable even among the hardy tribesmen of his own race, while his personal courage was proved in many a grim encounter with his adversaries. These virtues were combined with an unflinching moral courage, which taught him to meet all the trials and chances of his chequered career with equanimity, to seek the truth at all hazards, and to cherish an abiding faith in the power and beneficence of God. A very Man indeed, "he stood bare, not cased in euphemistic coat of mail; he grappled like a giant, face to face, heart to heart, with the naked truth of things." That after all is the sort of man one needs in a world of imitative mediocrities.

Babur's social qualities in no wise belied his princely descent. The pages of his *Memoirs* reveal many an instance of his consideration for dependents, his steady loyalty to old friends and old scenes, his love for his mother and respect for his womenfolk, his benevolence and his genial humour. He was "bon camarade" to all whom he liked and trusted, no matter whether they were the companions of his *symposia*, reclining at ease in one of his favourite "paradises" at Kabul, or were his soldiers, huddled together in the bitter snowstorm of the Zirrin Pass. "In the company of friends Death is a feast," he writes, and he declines the offer of warmth and shelter, in order to sit with his frozen men in the very grip of the storm! No wonder they loved him—those rude Mongols: he inspired them with the same blind devotion which brought *Les Vieux de la Vieille* in Gautier's ballad to do homage at the tomb of Napoleon. It was that devotion which enabled Babur again and again to achieve victory in most unfavourable conditions and against heavy odds.

Throughout his stormy career Babur's chief relaxation—his constant antidote to depression—was literary composition, which was often undertaken in the most uncompromising circumstances. The man who could compose an ode, while toiling over the mountains without adequate shelter, when the horses died of exhaustion and the rains flooded the tents knee-deep, may surely be said to have possessed in full measure the spirit of the philosopher. Almost to the last hour of his life Babur's intellectuality illumines like a golden thread the tale of his political fortunes. Of prose and poetry alike he was an accomplished student; and he bade his pen indite not only the imperishable annals of his military achievements, but also those incisive portraits of persons and descriptions of places, which reveal his quick eye for facts and mark him out as one of the most accomplished and cultivated Asiatic princes known to history. Not the least attractive feature of his character was his intense love of Nature and his delight in all the wonder and glory of the world. "The heart of Napoleon" it has been said, "thrilled to the appeal of great open spaces, to the mysterious sound of the sea, to the serene charm of pure starlit skies. But he would not notice the little unobtrusive beauties of Nature, the poise or tint of a flower, the song of a bird, the winter tracery of a tree; and if noticed, would have dismissed them like the plays of Racine, as elegancies fit only for young people." Therein lies the difference between the great Corsican and Babur; for the latter was always observant of even the smallest masterpieces of Nature's art. The colour of an autumn leaf, the hue of a tulip, the scent of a melon, sufficed to arouse his admiration and emotion ; while his love of flowers, as has been mentioned, led to his introducing into India the terraced gardens or pleasaunces, which have been described by a modern writer as the greatest contribution of the Mughals to Indian art.

Napoleon indeed lacked Babur's most precious possession—a deep and genuine sincerity, which is the first characteristic of all men in any way heroic. It was that quality which carried him unspotted and unscathed through the turmoil of the early years of his Kingship, which taught him to eschew any act savouring of infidelity or treachery, which rendered him immune from the worst vices of his age and race, and urged him to true repentance for temporary transgressions of the strict precepts of Islam. And lastly, it was that quality which endeared him alike to the comrades of his own rank and station, to the people of the Central Asian marts, and to the rough tribesmen who fought beneath his standard and laid the foundations of the splendid empire which his grandson, Akbar, finally perfected. Babur belonged to an age of great rulers—the age of Charles V, Francis I, Henry VIII and Suleiman the Magnificent; and one is inclined to regard him, the child of the Central Asian steppes, as in some ways the greatest and most attractive of them all.

TAMAM

The New Book of Trees

By MARCUS WOODWARD, author of *Country Contentments*, etc. With many Woodcuts by C. DILLON McGURK.

A unique tree book by "the modern Richard Jefferies." It will appeal alike to botanist, country squire, student of folklore, and the simple lover of Nature.

Demy 8vo. 12s. 6*d. net.*

Birds of Marsh and Mere, and How to Shoot them

By J. C. M. NICHOLS. Introductory Note by J. G. MILLAIS. Illustrated by the Author.

These notes of an experienced wildfowler contain invaluable information and advice regarding the shooting of geese, ducks and waders.

Demy 8vo. 15s. *net.*

Memoirs of a Child

By BASIL MACDONALD HASTINGS. With 50 Drawings by G. L. STAMPA.

Introduces an extremely naughty but most attractive family of eleven children.

7½ by 5½. 8*s.* 6*d. net.*

A Winter in Paradise

By ALAN PARSONS. Illustrated with 50 Photographs taken by the author.

An amusing diary recording the experiences of Mr. Parsons, his wife (Miss Viola Tree) and Lady Diana Cooper on a winter visit to the Bahamas, Cuba and Florida.

7½ by 5½. 7*s.* 6*d. net.*

The "Fourth" of the *Fernandina*

By GEORGE F. KNOX, Engineer-Lieutenant-Commander Royal Navy (Special Reserve).

A stirring record of a voyage across two oceans in the engine-room of a pre-war cargo steamer.

Crown 8vo. 7*s.* 6*d. net.*

Memoirs of a Poor Devil

By T. MURRAY FORD (THOMAS LE BRETON), author of *A Sister to Assist 'er, The Confessions of Mrs. May, Jo Crupper: Bus Conductor*, etc.

"A host of personal anecdotes of the people most talked about."—*Bystander.*

Demy 8vo. *Frontispiece.* 8*s.* 6*d. net.*

Gilles de Rais: the Original Bluebeard

By A. L. VINCENT and CLARE BINNS. Introduction by M. HAMBLIN SMITH, M.A., M.D.

A study of the amazing career, crimes and ruin of Joan of Arc's companion in arms.
"A vivid portrait of one of the greatest fiends of history."—*Bookman.*

7½ by 5½. *7 illustrations.* *8s. 6d. net.*

An Island Hell: a Soviet Prison in the Far North

By S. A. MALSAGOFF. Translated by F. H. LYON.

"Perhaps the most terrible indictment of the Bolshevist regime which has yet been penned."—*Evening Standard.*

Crown 8vo. *5s. net.*

The Tcheka: The Red Inquisition

Second Impression.

By GEORGE POPOFF.

"A terrible indictment of a terrible institution."—The Right Hon. Sir WILLIAM JOYNSON-HICKS, M.P.
"More exciting than any novel of adventure."—*The Times.*

Demy 8vo. *Frontispiece.* *8s. 6d. net.*

The Private Memoirs and Confessions of a Justified Sinner

New Edition.

By JAMES HOGG (1770-1835). With an Introduction by T. EARLE WELBY.

"A Grand Guignol book of genius. A revelation of spiritual horror too great for silence."—James Agate in the *Daily Graphic.*
"A genuine find. A masterpiece of the mystical and macabre."—Arthur Waugh in the *Daily Telegraph.*

Crown 8vo. *5s. net.*

Memories of a Singer

By MINNIE HAUK (BARONESS DE WARTEGG). Preface by A. M. WILLIAMSON (MRS. C. N. WILLIAMSON).

The life-story of the famous American *prima donna* who "invented" Carmen and revolutionised the dramatic side of opera.
"A kaleidoscope of vivid pictures."—*Morning Post.*

Demy 8vo. *16 illustrations.* *15s. net.*

French Cameos

By MOMA CLARKE, author of *Paris Waits*, etc.

"A work that every traveller to France, every visitor to Paris, should stand on his bookshelf."—*Illustrated Sporting and Dramatic News*.

7½ by 5½. | 90 *illustrations by A. Pécoud.* | 8*s.* 6*d. net.*

Arnold Bennett

Second Impression.

By MRS. ARNOLD BENNETT.

"I cannot think of any other author's wife who could have painted her famous husband with half the skill."—S. P. B. Mais in the *Daily Graphic*.

"Should be read by all who would know the real Arnold Bennett."—*Newcastle Chronicle*.

Crown 8vo. | 10 *illustrations.* | 7*s.* 6*d. net.*

The Last Years of Rodin

By MARCELLE TIREL. Translated by R. FRANCIS. Introduction by JUDITH CLADEL, author of *Rodin : l'Homme et l'Œuvre*, etc.

"Gives us a much more credible and intimate picture of the man than we have had before."—*Times Literary Supplement*.

7½ by 5½. | 4 *illustrations.* | 7*s.* 6*d. net.*

Adolphe

By BENJAMIN CONSTANT. Translated from the French by PAUL HOOKHAM. Introduction by GUSTAVE RUDLER, Marshal Foch Professor in the University of Oxford. Frontispiece portrait of the author.

The story of Constant's famous love-affair with Madame de Staël.

"A masterpiece . . . true and sound and revealing."—*Spectator*.

Edition de Luxe of 500 *numbered copies.* | 10*s.* 6*d. net.*

Figs from Thistles

By T. EARLE WELBY, author of *A Popular History of English Poetry*, etc.

An incisive criticism of modern democracy, which the writer declares to be peculiarly unsuited to the British people.

"One of the most suggestive and interesting little books that we have read for some time."—*Sheffield Daily Telegraph*.

Crown 8vo. | 5*s. net.*